Artists: Penko Gelev

Sotir Gelev

Editors: Stephen Haynes, Sophie Izod, Karen Smith
Editorial Assistant: Mark Williams

Published in Great Britain in MMXIII by
Book House, an imprint of
The Salariya Book Company Ltd
25 Marlborough Place, Brighton, BNI IUB
www.salariya.com
www.book-house.co.uk
ISBN-13: 978-1-908973-19-1

SALARIYA

A CIP catalogue record for this book is available
from the British Library.

Printed and bound in China.
Printed on paper from sustainable sources.

Visit our website at **www.salariya.com**
for **free** electronic versions of:
You Wouldn't Want to be an Egyptian Mummy!
You Wouldn't Want to be a Roman Gladiator!
You Wouldn't Want to be a Polar Explorer!
You Wouldn't Want to sail on a 19th-Century Whaling Ship!

Visit our **new** online shop at
shop.salariya.com
for great offers, gift ideas, all our new
releases and free postage and packaging.

Adventures at Sea

Treasure Island   Moby Dick   Robinson Crusoe

SALARIYA BH BOOK HOUSE

Treasure Island

Robert Louis Stevenson

Illustrated by
Penko Gelev

Retold by
Fiona Macdonald

Series created and designed by
David Salariya

If schooners, islands, and maroons,
And buccaneers, and buried gold,
And all the old romance, retold

Exactly in the ancient way,
Can please, as me they pleased of old,
The wiser youngsters of today:
So be it, and fall on!

Robert Louis Stevenson, Treasure Island

CHARACTERS

Jim Hawkins

Long John Silver,
an old sea-cook

Doctor Livesey

Captain Smollett,
Captain of the *Hispaniola*

Billy Bones,
an old sea-captain

Ben Gunn,
a marooned man

Squire Trelawney,
a wealthy gentleman

Blind Pew,
pirate

Tom Redruth,
gamekeeper

Israel Hands,
coxswain

Jim's
mother

Tom Morgan,
crewman

Job Anderson,
crewman

Abraham Gray,
crewman

Mr. Arrow,
first mate

Black Dog,
pirate

Dick Johnson,
crewman

George Merry,
crewman

John Hunter,
crewman

O'Brien,
crewman

8

STRANGER AT THE INN

All is quiet at the Admiral Benbow Inn – until a tall, weather-beaten stranger knocks at the door. It is Billy Bones, an old sea-captain.

Billy Bones calls for rum and asks lots of questions.[1] (see notes below) When he hears that the Inn has few visitors, he decides to stay for a while.

Jim, the landlord's son, has never seen anyone like Billy Bones. He's very curious about him.

All day, everyday, Billy Bones stares silently out to sea. What's he looking for? Who's he waiting for? And why is he so nervous?

Billy Bones asks Jim to warn him when strangers arrive at the Inn – especially if they are sailors.

Thinking about mysterious strangers gives Jim nightmares. He dreams of monsters and murderers.

Every night, Billy Bones tells tales of his adventures at sea. He's often drunk, and very rowdy.

Jim's father falls ill, so Doctor Livesey visits the Inn. He tells Billy Bones to behave better – Billy Bones is furious, and threatens him.

1. rum: A strong alcoholic drink.
2. weather-eye: To keep a close watch.

THE ADMIRAL BENBOW

Billy Bones patrols the cliffs.

I must be able to see any enemies approaching.

Jim is alone when a stranger enters the Inn. It is Black Dog, an out-of-work sailor. He calls for rum – and asks about Billy Bones.

We'll give Bill a little surprise . . .

Jim is suspicious. He tries to warn Billy Bones. But Black Dog stops him.

Well, then, speak up; what is it?

No, no, no, no.

When Billy Bones returns to the Inn, he finds Black Dog waiting for him. He goes pale with shock but recovers quickly.

Black Dog tells Billy to sit down. They call for rum, and send Jim away so he can't listen to their conversation. All of a sudden, a fierce quarrel breaks out.

If it comes to swinging, swing all, say I.[1]

They fight.

Are you hurt?

We'll be back to get you, Billy Bones!

I must get away from here.

Black Dog runs away, clutching his wounded shoulder. Billy Bones looks shaken.

He asks Jim for more rum. Jim hurries to fetch the drink. But while he's away, Billy Bones collapses. The noise has alarmed Jim's mother who comes running in to help.

1. swinging: Being hanged.

Jim's mother calls Doctor Livesey. He tells Billy Bones, he's had a stroke and needs to rest quietly.[2]

While Billy Bones recovers, he tells Jim about his life at sea. He says Black Dog and his old shipmates want to steal his treasure.

Suddenly, sadness strikes Jim's family. His father falls ill, and dies. Now Jim is so busy he doesn't have time to worry about Billy.

While Jim and his mother mourn, Billy Bones helps himself to rum. It makes him even more fearful. He sits brooding, with sword in hand.

Then, one day, a mysterious blind beggar arrives at the Inn. He seems weak and helpless. But really, he's tough and cruel. Billy seems helpless to refuse his orders.

Blind Pew presses a small square of paper into Billy Bones's hand. The effect is alarming.

Billy leaps to his feet and cries out his defiance to Jim. But even as he does so, he clutches his hand to his throat and falls to the floor.

Jim tries to help him, but it's too late – Billy Bones is dead! He's been killed by thundering apoplexy.[3] Even though Jim didn't like him, he had begun to feel sorry for Billy.

1. The name of rum for you is death: Drinking rum will kill him.
2. stroke: When a blood vessel inside the brain is damaged causing the person to lose consciousness.
3. apoplexy: Another term for having a stroke. It also means a fit of extreme anger.

BILLY BONES'S SEA-CHEST

Quick, before they return!

But I'll go and get the Doctor – and some other help too![1]

Jim and his mother rush out of the Inn, leaving Billy Bones dead on the floor. Where can they go? What can they do?

They hurry to the nearest village, and ask for help to arrest Blind Pew. But no one is brave enough!

What's this in his hand?

It's opening!

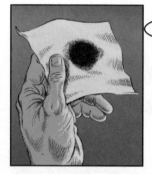

Fearfully, Jim and his mother creep back to the Inn. There's no sign of Blind Pew. But Billy Bones's body is still there.

It's the Black Spot! It warned Billy that he had until ten o'clock that night before the pirates came for the treasure.

Jim also finds a key, hung around Billy's neck. His mother tries it in the lock of the old sea-chest Billy brought to the Inn.

I'll have my dues, and not a farthing over.[2]

Down with the door!

The chest contains clothes, a compass, guns – and very smelly tobacco. Hidden right at the bottom, there's a small, heavy bag and a mysterious packet.

Jim takes the packet. His mother opens the bag. It's full of real gold coins – more than enough to pay Billy's debts!

Suddenly, Jim hears a sinister, scary sound – a stick tap-tap-tapping at the Inn's front door. Blind Pew is back . . . and he's not alone.

1. The Doctor is also the local judge so would be able to help them. There was no police force at this time.
2. farthing: An old coin used in England in the 18th century.

"Take the money and run."

Jim and his mother have to run for their lives. Jim's mother soon gets tired, and collapses. Jim helps her to hide under a bridge.

"Aloft and get the chest."

Meanwhile, back at the Inn, Blind Pew and his gang are smashing their way through the door. They are armed with deadly weapons.

"Is it there?"

"They've been before us!"

"Someone's turned the chest out.."

They rush to Billy's room, to get his sea-chest. They find it, open – and empty!

"Scatter and find 'em! Rout the house out![1]"

Thump!

Bang!

Crash!

Crack!

The furious gang destroys the Inn.

Suddenly they hear a blast from their lookout warning them that the Coastguard patrol are closing in on them.

"You won't leave old Pew mates – not old Pew!"

"Run for your lives!"

"Back to our boat!"

"Aaaaaaaarghhh!!!"

The gang hear the Coastguards approaching, and escape. But they leave Blind Pew behind. Without them, he is helpless and stumbles into the path of a Coastguard's horse.

"They'll be hunting for this packet."

"Let's ask the Doctor what to do."

With Pew dead and the rest of the gang escaped, peace returns. But Jim is still worried. He warns the guards that the gang may come back.

1. rout the house: Search the house.

BURIED TREASURE

He's visiting Squire Trelawney, sir!

Is Dr Livesey in?

What good wind brings you here?

Come in.

Jim and the guards arrive at the Doctor's house but discover he is not at home. They ride on to the Hall, and find the Doctor and the Squire talking by the fireside.[1]

Blind Pew won't trouble us again!

But his gang might come back any day!

Here it is, sir.

It's a list of Billy Bones's pirate loot!

The Coastguard tells the Squire about Blind Pew and his gang. Then he goes home, leaving Jim behind at the Hall.

Jim shows the Squire the mysterious packet he found in Billy Bones's sea-chest.

The Squire and the Doctor examine the packet. They cut the strings that fasten it, and open it very carefully. Inside, they find a book . . .

He was the blood-thirstiest buccaneer that sailed.[2]

Look at this, it says, "Bulk of treasure here"!

Will that treasure amount to much?

. . . and a map of a tropical island! The map is marked with compass directions and three red crosses.[3] The Squire peers at these closely then shouts out in excitement.

The Squire soon realises they've found the infamous Captain Flint's treasure map.

Captain Flint was the cruellest, cleverest, richest pirate who ever sailed the seas, and his treasure must be worth a fortune!

14 1. Squire: The title given to the main landowner in an area. It's no longer used.
2. buccaneer: Another name for a pirate.

In three weeks time we'll have the best ship in England . . . Hawkins shall be cabin-boy.

This is Redruth, the Squire's gamekeeper. He'll look after you.

The Squire gets very excited, and makes plans for an expedition. He'll buy a ship, hire a crew, and dig up Captain Flint's treasure!

The next day, the Squire leaves for Bristol, the nearest big port. The Doctor goes to care for his patients, Jim stays behind at the Hall.

He's got a ship!

Jim is happy at the Hall. He feels safe from Blind Pew's gang. He spends his time studying Captain Flint's treasure map and dreaming of adventure.

One day, Jim gets a letter from the Squire. It contains thrilling news – the Squire has bought a ship: the *Hispaniola*.

Farewell, my son! Take care!

Don't cry, Mother.

In the letter, the Squire also says that the Doctor is in London and will meet them in Bristol. He tells Jim to hurry and join them.

Jim is very excited, but his mother can't help worrying if she will ever see him again. So Jim sets out for Bristol, with trusty Redruth beside him as protection.

What will he find there? Who will he meet? And will he enjoy his adventure? As he says goodbye to his home, Jim spares a thought for poor Billy Bones.

LONG JOHN SILVER

It's like another world.

Jim and Redruth arrive in Bristol, and make their way to the harbour. They have never seen such fine ships – or seen so many strange looking people.

We sail tomorrow!

They find the Squire and the Doctor waiting for them. The Squire is in high spirits. He announces that he's hired a crew and the adventure will begin in the morning.

Billy Bones was scared of a one-legged sailor. Long John can't be the same man – can he?

Pleased to meet you, Jim lad!

Long John welcomes Jim to his neat,. clean Inn. He seems kind and friendly. Jim soon forgets his worries – this can't be the man Billy feared!

Stop him! It's Black Dog!

The next day, Jim is sent to fetch Long John Silver, the ship's new cook. The Squire tells him Silver only has one leg and as Jim walks along the docks he worries this is the man Billy Bones was so scared of.

But who's this, lurking in a dark corner? It's Black Dog, the old shipmate who threatened Billy Bones! When he sees Jim, he heads for the door and is soon outside and running.

Black Dog hadn't paid his bill, so Long John Silver sends two barmen to chase him. He seems very surprised to learn a pirate has been visiting his Inn.

The barmen return, empty-handed. They've bad news to report – Black Dog got away! Silver tells Jim how ashamed he is he couldn't catch Black Dog himself.

Silver says he'll go with Jim to see the Squire. As they walk along, he talks about the ships they see in the harbour.

Silver tells the Squire how Black Dog ran away from his Inn. He is anxious that the Squire won't think he's friendly with pirates.

Later, the Squire and the Doctor discuss Long John Silver. They both like him, and are looking forward to setting sail.

1. keel-haul: Being dragged through the water and along the underside (keel) of a ship.

THE ADVENTURE BEGINS

The ship is ready!

This is so exciting!

Jim goes on board with the Squire and the Doctor. They are welcomed by Mr. Arrow, the first mate.[1] A weather-beaten old sailor, he's second-in-command and seems honest.

I don't like this cruise; I don't like the men and I don't like my officer.

I've heard you have a map of an island . . .

I never told that to a soul!

Next, they meet Captain Smollett. He's brisk, stern and clever. In the past, he's led many successful voyages. But right now, he's angry!

The Squire has not yet told the Captain of his plans to find Flint's treasure. But the crew seem to know all about it.

Let me take certain precautions or let me resign.

You fear a mutiny?[2]

If the crewmen know too much, they'll take the treasure for themselves!

The Captain is horrified when he hears the Squire's plans. He warns that treasure-hunting is very risky. They might all be killed!

The Captain agrees to stay. But he warns they must hide the map of the island, and keep all their plans secret from the crew, if they can.

1. first mate: The officer on a ship who is second-in-command to the captain.
2. mutiny: When the crew of a ship rebel and take control from the captain.

Jim watches as the crew hoist the sails and load the ship with food and water. They'll sail on the next tide.

Soon, a friendly face peers over the ship's side. It's Long John Silver! As he scrambles on board, the crew hurry to greet him.

Long John salutes Captain Smollett, who orders him below decks to start cooking straight away.

At last the stores are all aboard, and it's time to leave port. The crewmen turn the heavy capstan that hauls up the anchor.[1]

To help them work, Long John Silver sings. Jim remembers that he's heard the song before – from the old pirate, Billy Bones!

---

1. capstan: The wheel that the anchor cable is wound around to either lower or raise the anchor.

OUTWARD VOYAGE

> But I still don't trust any of them – except perhaps the Doctor.

Their long journey starts well, with fine weather and calm seas. The ship sails south and west, out into the Atlantic Ocean.

Jim enjoys life on board. The crew are friendly, the Captain is an excellent commander, and even Silver's cooking tastes good!

> Wretched man.

> Hic! Slurp!

> Aieeeeeeeeeeeeeeeeeeeee!

> Steady as she goes.

Most of the crew work hard, but Mr. Arrow is drunk for most of the time. One night he disappears and it's assumed that he's fallen overboard.

Mr. Arrow is replaced by two senior crewmen: Job Anderson and Israel Hands. They take over the important task of steering the ship.

> I've seen him fight four men at once!

> Come and have a yarn with John.[1]

Hands is an old friend of Silver's. They've often sailed together. He says Silver is fierce and strong – and as brave as a lion. The entire crew seems to like and respect him, including Jim.

Silver is always pleased to see Jim and loves to talk about great sailors and epic voyages. He describes rich treasure-ships, laden with silks, spices, jewels and golden coins.

1. yarn: A seafaring term for talking.

Pieces of eight!
Pieces of eight![1]

Something's not right,
I fear trouble.

I call her 'Captain Flint',
after the famous buccaneer.
He was wicked!

Silver says his parrot is 200 years old, and has spent her life at sea. Like him, she's seen battles, shipwrecks, and tonnes of treasure!

Jim is happy – though he wonders why the name 'Captain Flint' makes him feel uneasy. But not everyone onboard is happy.

Spoil forecastle hands,
make devils.[2]

Squire says we can
help ourselves!

The Squire and the Captain still don't like each other. They frequently quarrel, and when the Squire gives the crew extra rations of cake and rum, the Captain becomes angry.

But the Squire ignores the Captain's advice, and offers the crew free apples. These are stored on deck in a huge wooden barrel.

I can reach them
if I climb inside.

I can hear voices,
there's someone
coming!

Yawn.

The voyage is going well and one evening when Jim has finished his work, he goes to fetch an apple. Finding there are not many left, he climbs in to reach the bottom.

There's lots of room inside, and it's a good place to shelter from wind and sea-spray. Jim eats his apple, then becomes sleepy from the rocking of the ship. He dozes off.

Suddenly, he awakes . . .

1. Pieces of eight: The name of an old Spanish silver coin.
2. The Captain warns that being too kind to the crew will stop them having respect for him.

MUTINY!

Flint was cap'n; I was quartermaster, along of my timber leg.[1]

I'll finish with them at the island as soon as the blunt's on board.[2]

The voices Jim hears belong to Silver, Israel Hands and Dick Johnson. To his horror he learns they were part of Flint's pirate crew!

They plan to mutiny, take over the ship and dispose of the Squire, Captain and Doctor. After that, they plan to keep Flint's treasure for themselves.

They'll kill us all!

It'll be like the good old days!

Wait is what I say, but when the time comes, let her rip!

Jim is still hiding inside the barrel, and what he hears fills him with terror. They're so cold-hearted! What will he do?

Hands wants to strike quickly, he's angry at having to follow the Captain's orders. Dick wonders if they should maroon the Squire and his friends or just kill them.[3]

Silver convinces Hands that it's much better to let Captain Smollett get them to the island, and to use the extra men to carry the treasure onboard before killing them.

Let's drink to luck . . . and old Flint.

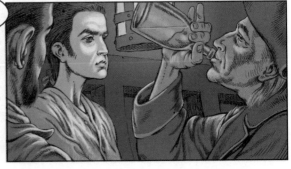

He warns the mutineers to keep their plans secret, until it's time take action.

Excited by their hopes of finding Captain Flint's treasure, the mutineers start drinking. They tell bloodthirsty stories of past pirate raids.

---

1. quartermaster: A low ranking officer responsible for steering a ship.
2. blunt: Treasure.
3. maroon: Abandoning someone on an island.

Not another man of them'll jine.[1]

Dick leaves, and Jim hears Hands whispering to Silver, he only manages to hear a few words of what is said, but what he does hear gives him hope.

There are still **some** faithful men on board.

There are some men on board that the pirates have not managed to turn against the Captain. But who can Jim trust?

Suddenly . . .

LAND HO!

. . . it were a main place for pirates once."

Skeleton Island they calls it . . .

It's the island! Everyone rushes up to the main deck to have a good look.

They want to kill you, too!

We're in terrible danger!

Doctor, I have terrible news.

We must go on, because we can't turn back.

While everyone else is busy looking at the island, Jim has a private word with the Doctor.

Jim tells the Doctor about the planned mutiny – and that most of the crew seem to be pirates!

The Doctor takes Jim straight to the Captain's cabin. Jim tells the Captain, Doctor and Squire all he has heard.

1. jine: Join.

TREASURE ISLAND

The ship sails on, closer to the island. Captain Smollett asks the crew what they know about Flint and his treasure. He wants to know who the pirates are, and who he can trust.

The Captain shows the crew a copy he has made of Billy Bones's map. The mutineers all pretend not to have seen it before. Silver must be disappointed it isn't Billy Bones's map, but he hides it well.

At dawn the next day, the island is clearly visible. To Jim it seems strange and desolate.[1]

The ship sails closer to the shore, then carefully drops anchor in the dangerous waters.

The mutineers among the crew are restless and surly. Silver tries to keep them in order, and is even more cheerful and helpful to the Captain.

The Captain tells the crew that they can go ashore – they are delighted. Meanwhile, he tells Hunter, Joyce and Redruth of the plot against them.

Thirteen of the crew climb into the boats and head for the island . . . but they leave six men behind on the *Hispaniola*.

The six mutineers are given orders to stay alert but not to act against the Captain without Silver's order.

1. desolate: Deserted and lifeless.

Like the crew, Jim wants to explore the island. He stows away on one of the boats, hoping that no-one will see him.[1]

But Silver quickly spots him, and is angry. Jim is scared and starts to regret his foolishness.

Jim, is that you?

As soon as the boats reach the shore, Jim leaps out, and runs to hide in the jungle. Silver calls out to him, but Jim keeps running.

Jim runs on and on . . .

Sounds like a spinning top.

He sees many giant plants and strange wild animals. In a forest clearing, he comes face to face with a deadly rattlesnake.

If I die like a dog, I'll die in my dooty.[2]

Suddenly Jim hears voices. It's Silver and one of the crewmen who refuses to mutiny. Silver tries to convince the man, but then in the distance they hear a terrible scream.

Silver pulls out his knife, and the terrified crewman starts to run away. But Silver is too fast, and throws a heavy branch that knocks him to the ground.

Aghast, Jim watches as Silver stabs him, the effort leaving him out of breath. Soon the poor crewman is dead.

Jim faints with the shock of witnessing this brutal murder. When he wakes, his mind is filled with fears that Silver will kill him too.

1. stow away: To hide on a ship.
2. dooty: Duty – the crewman will not betray Captain Smollett.

BEN GUNN

Jim gets up, and starts running. He's filled with terror and desperate to get away from Long John Silver.

A sudden sound makes Jim stop, terrified. He looks ahead and sees a shadowy shape leaping through the trees.

Luckily Jim remembers his gun! The Captain gave it to him when he heard of the crew's plans to mutiny. Now Jim bravely steps forward.

Slowly the shadowy shape comes closer. Could it be a cannibal? No, it's a wild and ragged looking man who begs Jim for mercy.

Kneeling, the man tells Jim that he's a British sailor, and his name is Ben Gunn.

Ben Gunn tells Jim that he's the first person he's spoken to in three long, lonely years.

He was marooned. Since then, his life has been hard and lonely, but he has survived.

He's made clothes from goatskins and old sails, a rough shelter and a little boat. Mysteriously, he also claims to have found a fortune!

So much I'll tell you and no more.

Ben Gunn explains that he was an old shipmate of Long John Silver, Billy Bones, Blind Pew and Captain Flint.

Flint and six of the crew went ashore to bury the treasure . . .

But, there he was, and the six all dead.

. . . but Flint returned alone.

Three years later when Ben saw the island with a different crew of pirates, he suggested they look for Flint's treasure. When they found nothing, they marooned him.

Not a man with one leg?

Jim tells Ben that some of Flint's old crew are on the island, and Ben reveals that he too is scared of Long John Silver.

Jim asks Ben Gunn to come with him to meet the Captain and the Squire. He knows they'll help Ben Gunn travel back to Britain and they can all share the treasure.

Ben Gunn has reasons of his own.

Ben Gunn is scared and runs away into the trees. But he tells Jim not to worry, and that he will find him again.

A Safe Shelter?

"What's this?"

Nervously, Jim heads back to the shore. On the way, he spots a wooden cabin, surrounded by a stockade.[1]

While Jim is talking to Ben Gunn, the Captain, Doctor and Squire take one of the boats and escape to shore. Abraham Gray struggles free from the pirates to rejoin his Captain.

The pirates on board try very hard to stop them. Israel Hands, who was Flint's gunner readies the cannon to shoot.[2]

The Squire is the best shot and tries to shoot Hands, but misses, hitting one of the other pirates instead.

BANG!
BOOM!
CRASH!

The pirates shoot at the Captain's jolly-boat, hoping to sink it.[3] But the loyal crew members, Hunter, Joyce, Redruth and Gray, row hard and steer them so that the cannon-balls land harmlessly in the sea.

"This way, men!"

As the boat reaches the island they wade ashore and head for the stockade. The captain knows how to find it from Billy Bones's map.

But the main gang of pirates is hiding nearby, ready to ambush and kill them. They attack!

"Be I going, Doctor?"

After a short gunfight, the pirates run away, but Redruth, the Squire's faithful gamekeeper, is fatally wounded.[4]

1. stockade: A camp or building surrounded by a fence or wall.
2. gunner: The person in charge of firing the cannons.
3. jolly-boat: A medium sized boat used to bring people ashore.
4. fatally wounded: Received an injury that will kill him.

The Captain leads the way to the cabin. Once there, they take stock of the provisions they've managed to save from the ship.

That will show them!

Captain Smollett takes the British flag from his pocket, and climbs to the roof to run it up in defiance of the pirates.[1]

The rations are very short.

Together, the Captain and the Doctor discuss food supplies. The consort could not be expected to reach them for several months.[2]

BOOM! BANG!

Their discussions are interrupted by cannon fire from the ship. They can't see the cabin, but are aiming at the flag! At this moment . . .

I am not sure whether he is sane.

. . . Jim leaps over the stockade to rejoin his friends. He describes his meeting with Ben Gunn, and repeats all that he has learned.

The Captain sets the loyal crewmen to work. The food supplies are so low the Captain is worried they'll be starved out.

Captain says it's good for us to keep busy.

The men dig a grave for their fallen shipmate, Redruth and gather plenty of firewood for cooking and warmth.

Sadly, they bury poor Tom Redruth – a good man killed in the struggle to get hold of Captain Flint's pirate treasure. Privately, each person wonders how many more will die.

1. run it up: Attaching a flag to a pole.
2. consort: The rescue ship which would be sent once it was noted the *Hispaniola* was late returning to Bristol.

Sworn Enemies

The Captain, Doctor and Squire meet to make plans. They decide to stay in the stockade, and kill the pirates one by one.

But the very next morning, Long John Silver arrives at the stockade waving a flag of truce.[1] He says he wants peace and is now using the name 'Captain' Silver!

These lads chose me cap'n after your desertion, sir.

We want that treasure, and we'll have it.

The Captain refuses to let Silver enter the cabin, but listens quietly as he offers the mutineer's peace terms: they want Billy Bones's map.

In return, they will let the Captain and his men back onboard the ship. They promise no harm will come to them.

No!

Refuse, and you've seen the last of me but musket-balls.

They sit on the ground and Silver tries to persuade him, but the Captain stays firm. When Silver issues threats, he orders the pirate out of the stockade.

Them that die'll be the lucky ones.

Silver asks for help to stand, but nobody comes forward. He's forced to crawl to the cabin where he can pull himself upright. He's furious and curses the Captain and his men.

I've no manner of doubt that we can drub them, if you choose.[2]

It's war! The Captain warns that the pirates will soon attack the stockade. He warns his men to prepare for the pirates.

1. truce: A temporary halt to fighting.
2. drub: Defeat.

30

The pirates surround the stockade. They are all armed with guns and deadly cutlasses.[1]

Inside, the Captain and his men get ready to fight for their lives.

The battle begins! The pirates rush over the stockade and charge towards the Captain's men.

Aaarggghhhhh!

Fight 'em in the open!

The fighting is fast and furious. Jim bravely takes part. Hunter is knocked unconscious, Joyce is sadly killed, but they manage to kill five of the pirates.

Look! The Captain's wounded!

Have they run?

At last the battle is over and the pirates limp away to their camp on the shore. But the Captain's men have suffered great losses and are still in danger . . .

1. Cutlasses: Short swords with curved blades used by pirates.

JIM'S SEA ADVENTURE

Next morning.

Hunter dies overnight, without waking. The Doctor tends the Captain's wounds, then sets off into the woods to try and find Ben Gunn.

During the night, Jim has also thought of a plan. He takes guns and food, and while the others are occupied . . .

. . . he climbs over the stockade and hurries to the shore. He wants to find Ben Gunn's boat, and escape from the island. He hides himself until nightfall.

Later that night.

Jim finds Ben Gunn's homemade boat, then sees the *Hispaniola* at anchor. It's flying the Jolly Roger![1]

With great difficulty, Jim carries Ben Gunn's little goatskin boat down to the water.

Jim climbs aboard, then paddles towards the ship. The sea is rough and Jim struggles to keep control. The coracle is safe, yet it has an alarming habit of twisting round and round in the water, which makes it hard to steer.[2]

Jim reaches the ship – and hacks away at the anchor rope until there are only a few strands left holding it.

1. Jolly Roger: The pirate flag. It was often a black background with a white skull and crossbones.
2. coracle: A small round boat made of material stretched over a wooden frame.

From above, Jim can hear the sound of men drinking and quarrelling. It's Hands and another man, O'Brien – both sound drunk.

At last, the rope breaks, and the ship floats free. The men on board have not noticed!

Quickly, Jim seizes his chance. grabs the end of the rope and climbs up it like a monkey!

Jim reaches the edge of the ship's main deck. Cautiously, he peers over. The watchmen are too busy fighting to notice.

Without an anchor, the ship floats free . . .

At last the mutineers onboard realise what is happening! They rush to the ship's side and peer over. What they see fills them with fear.

Jim fears the men will see him. So he climbs back down into Ben Gunn's boat, and falls asleep exhausted, to dream of the Admiral Benbow Inn.

33

DEADLY PERIL

The next morning.

Jim sleeps for hours – and wakes to find himself surrounded by high waves. Ben Gunn's boat bobs and swirls uncontrollably.

Worse still, strange monsters are lurking close to the shore. To Jim, they look like giant slugs, but he finds out later that they're harmless sea-lions!

That's our ship! Adrift! It's coming this way!

Jim leaps for his life as the ship crashes into Ben Gunn's boat. He scrambles on board . . .

Brandy.

. . . where a terrible sight meets his eyes: two men, both covered in blood. One is dead, the other is still alive . . . just. He manages to utter only one word.

What a mess!

The living man is Israel Hands, one of the leading pirates. Feeling sorry for the dying man, Jim goes to fetch him some brandy.

I've come aboard to take possession of this ship.

Hands sits up and drinks, but he's still very weak. Jim seizes the chance to take control.

And there's an end to Captain Silver!

He hauls the pirates' Jolly Roger down from the mast. Jim and the wounded pirate strike a deal to help each other.

Jim tries to steer the ship to safety, and grumbling all the time, Israel Hands tells him what to do. They sail the *Hispaniola* along the coast of the island.

Jim dresses Hands's wounds and the pirate starts to recover. When he thinks Jim's not looking he grabs a short dirk.[2] Jim notices that Hands often watches him carefully.

Together, Jim and Hands steer the ship towards the shore. Hands issues orders for landing the ship and Jim is kept busy . . .

. . . but something makes him turn and he sees Hands advancing, dirk in hand. He's been pretending to be weaker than he is! As he attacks, Jim runs up the mizzen-shrouds.[3]

Hands climbs after him but his wounded leg makes progress slow and painful. This gives Jim time to load his guns. But Hands throws a knife that hits Jim in the shoulder.

Panicked, Jim fires his guns and Hands cries out, losing his hold.

Hands falls into the sea, dead. Jim feels sick and terrified, but finds the strength to climb down from the rigging.

Luckily his wound is not serious because Jim must now steer the ship alone, and try to reach dry land safely.

He loses control and the ship runs aground. Jim climbs off, and heads inland to try to find the Captain, Squire and Doctor . . . if they are still alive.

1. Dead men don't bite: Dead men are no danger.
2. dirk: A dagger.
3. mizzen-shrouds: The ropes attached to the mizzen mast.

ENEMY CAMP

"What might it be?"

"They keep an infamous bad watch."

Jim walks inland. What's that red glow he can see? Surely Ben Gunn isn't being so careless with his cooking fire . . .

Keeping low, Jim creeps up to the cabin in the centre of the stockade. He's amazed that nobody appears to be keeping lookout.

He hears men snoring and tiptoes quietly inside, expecting to find the Captain, Doctor and Squire.

"Pieces of eight! Pieces of eight!"

"So, here's Jim Hawkins, shiver my timbers!"

But suddenly, Jim finds himself surrounded by pirates! They've taken over the stockade. The Captain, Doctor and Squire are now sheltering in Ben Gunn's cave.

Long John Silver demands to know what Jim's been doing since they last met.

"You'll have to jine with Cap'n Silver."

"If you want to know who did it – it was I!"

"Avast, there!"

"Then here goes!"

He says that the Captain, Doctor and Squire are angry with Jim for running off without a word and leaving them. Jim's horrified that his friends have turned against him.

He confesses that he's been behind all the pirates' failures: the men left onboard are dead and the *Hispaniola's* adrift!

When the pirates hear this, they become very angry. They want to kill Jim straight away, but Silver persuades them to spare the boy.

The pirates are furious with Silver for protecting Jim from their revenge. They turn on him, sneering and cursing. They threaten him, but Silver is unafraid and dares them to attack him.

The pirates huddle together and hold a council of war. Every now and then they look over to where Silver and Jim are standing.

Silver tells Jim that both their lives are in danger and the pirates are now both their enemies. He promises to save Jim, if in turn Jim saves him from hanging.

The pirates decide to give Silver the Black Spot which they cut from a Bible. Silver turns the paper over and sees the word 'Deposed'.

Like Billy Bones before him, Silver knows he is in trouble and must think quickly to survive.

But he's clever and brave, and argues with the pirates about why he should stay Captain. Eventually he strikes a deal with them.

If they spare his life – and Jim's – Silver will give them Billy Bones's treasure map. The Doctor handed it to him when he left the stockade. The pirates can't believe their luck, and they leap upon the map, cheering and praising Long John Silver.

1. Deposed: No longer wanted as Captain.

The Skeleton's Secret

Daybreak next morning.

Next day, the Doctor calls at the stockade. He's come to check on the wounded pirates and is amazed to find Jim there. After the Doctor has treated the men, he says he wants to talk to Jim alone.

Silver tells him that he must step outside the stockade while he and Jim talk. He also tells the Doctor how he saved Jim and seems to be trying to be friendly.

The Doctor tells Jim he must try to escape. He wants him to jump over the fence and make a run for freedom. But Jim gave his word not to escape and has to refuse.

The Doctor tells Jim that they've found Ben Gunn, and then gives him a mysterious warning . . .

Then he walks away, to join the Captain and the Squire, back in Ben Gunn's cave. He tells Silver to keep Jim close to him.

Now they've got the map, the pirates are desperate to dig up Captain Flint's treasure.

They tie a rope around Jim which Silver holds, leading him like a dancing bear.

They row along the coast . . .

. . . then march inland, using clues marked on Billy Bones's map to guide them.

They find the the first clue – a tall pine tree – but then they find a horrid surprise!

They see the skeleton of a man stretched out on the ground. He seems to be lying in an odd way, almost as if he was pointing to something . . .

The dead man must be one of the six men killed by Captain Flint. The pirates remember how cruel he was.

But then they're terrified to hear a thin, eerie voice singing. They believe it's the ghost of wicked Captain Flint come to haunt them!

(It's really Ben Gunn, hiding in the bushes!)

As they're fleeing, Silver calls them back.

Silver convinces them that it wasn't Flint they heard, and they all hurry on to the spot where Captain Flint buried his treasure. But when they arrive they find an empty hole . . . the treasure's gone!

1. gone below: Gone to Hell.

HEADING HOME

The pirates are dumbstruck. They howl with rage and fury and quickly turn against Silver again. As they raise their weapons and advance, Jim thinks there is no hope.

But then there's a blaze of gunfire from the bushes behind them. Some pirates fall to the ground. Jim and Long John Silver survive!

It's the Doctor, Abe Gray and Ben Gunn who have been hiding in the bushes with their guns. The Doctor is eager to stop the pirates' escaping.

The remaining pirates make a run for the shore, followed by Jim, Silver and the Doctor.

As they hurry along, Ben Gunn tells Silver how he discovered the treasure by accident one day.

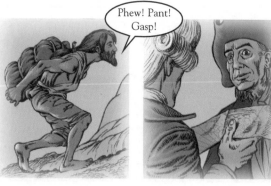

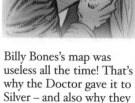

He discovered the treasure years ago, dug it up, and carried it sack by sack, up to his cave.

Billy Bones's map was useless all the time! That's why the Doctor gave it to Silver – and also why they abandoned the stockade!

Now Jim must help his friends find the *Hispaniola* so they can carry all of Flint's treasure back to England. They set off in the jolly-boat to row along the coast.

As they look up to the cliffs by Ben's cave they see the Squire waiting to greet them. They cheer with happiness, including Long John.

They find the *Hispaniola* drifting close to the shore. It's slightly damaged, but still seaworthy.

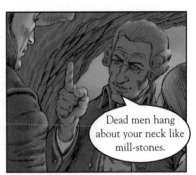

Dead men hang about your neck like mill-stones.

Silver salutes the Squire which angers him, and he makes his dislike of the cunning old pirate very clear. But as Silver saved Jim, the Squire has agreed not to prosecute him.

The Squire says Silver must help load the ship with treasure. Jim wonders how much blood has been spilled for the gold.

Nearly every variety of money in the world must be here.

Jim helps by sorting the glittering gold coins into bulging, clinking sackfuls. There are gold coins from all over the world.

Don't go!

We're maroooooooned!

Soon it's time to go. They leave the remaining three pirates behind. The Captain can't risk another mutiny and if they returned to England, they'd be hanged anyway.

As for the wily pirate, Long John Silver, he is a friendly and helpful sea-cook again. But, at their first port of call in South America, he escapes with a sackful of gold and is never seen again.

Jim, Ben Gunn, the Captain, Doctor and Squire arrive safely back in Bristol and share out the remaining gold. But Jim can't forget all he's done, or seen and no power in Heaven or Earth could make him go back to the island which still haunts his most terrifying nightmares.

The End

MOBY DICK

HERMAN MELVILLE

Illustrated by
Penko Gelev

Retold by
Sophie Furse

Series created and designed by
David Salariya

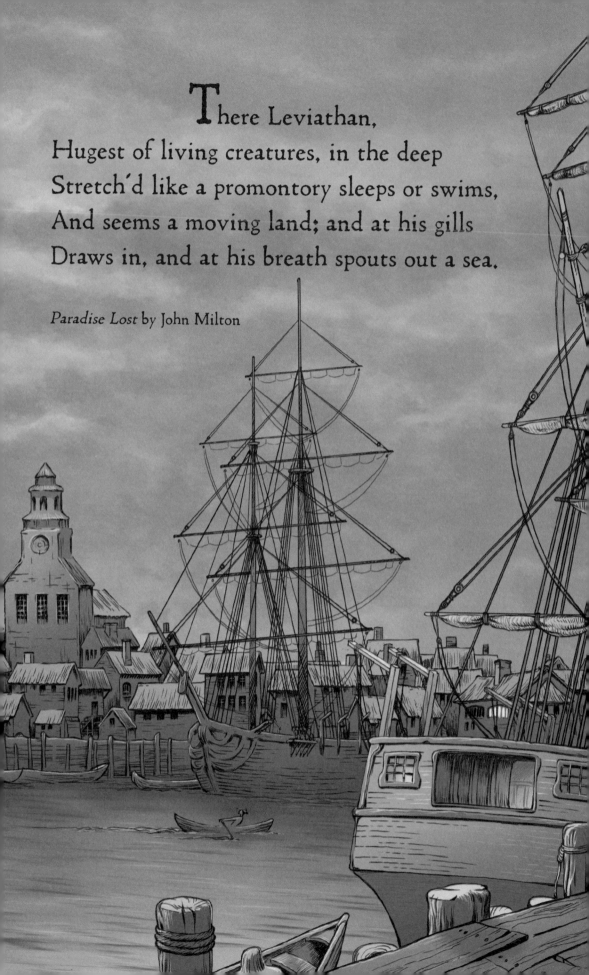

There Leviathan,
Hugest of living creatures, in the deep
Stretch'd like a promontory sleeps or swims,
And seems a moving land; and at his gills
Draws in, and at his breath spouts out a sea.

Paradise Lost by John Milton

CHARACTERS

Ishmael,
the narrator

Captain Ahab,
captain of the
Pequod

Queequeg,
harpooner

Stubb,
second mate

Fedallah

Mrs Hussey,
owner of
The Try Pots Inn

Starbuck,
first mate

Tashtego,
harpooner

Captain Peleg,
co-owner of
the *Pequod*

Captain
Bildad,
co-owner of
the *Pequod*

Daggoo,
harpooner

Elijah,
a mysterious stranger

Flask,
third mate

Perth,
blacksmith

"CALL ME ISHMAEL"

It was a cold Saturday night when I arrived in New Bedford. I was on my way to Nantucket to join the crew of a whaling ship.

I heard a forlorn creaking and saw a sign outside The Spouter Inn.

The landlord told me I would have to share a bed with a harpooner. The night was bitter and I decided it better to share half a decent man's blanket than go elsewhere.

I was awoken by the arrival of the mysterious harpooner, carrying a candle in one hand and a bag in the other.

I was just summoning my courage to speak to him, when he blew out the candle, lit his pipe and leapt into bed! By now, sure he was a cannibal, I cried out in terror.

The landlord appeared and reassured me that Queequeg had no desire to eat me so, mind at rest, I fell asleep.

In the morning, Queequeg leapt out of bed and told me he would dress first and leave me alone. He began to shave using not a razor, but his harpoon!

Breakfast was served and the other boarders all appeared to be whalemen judging by their dress and tanned faces. Ignoring the bread and coffee the others were eating, my room-mate reached over the table with his harpoon and speared a piece of bloody, almost raw meat.

CHRISTIANS AND CANNIBALS

It being a Sunday, I decided to visit the Whaleman's Chapel. I strolled through the town, noting the houses of the wealthy, all paid for with profits from whaling.

Sleet was soon driving down. I followed the procession of sailors, sailor's wives and sailor's widows into the chapel.

Yes, Ishmael, the same fate may be thine.[1]

I took my seat and looked around, surprised to see Queequeg. I began to read the marble memorials to the men lost at sea and felt saddened.

God had prepared a great fish to swallow up Jonah.

The doors opened and the legendary Father Mapple entered, shaking sleet from his coat.[2] (see notes below)

He took his place in the ship-like pulpit, and delivered a passionate sermon on the fitting subject of Jonah and the whale.[3]

Later on, I returned to the inn and found Queequeg there alone. Finding him considerably less terrifying by the light of day, I decided to get to know him better.

As we became better acquainted, Queequeg made me a gift of a shrunken head. A strange and ugly gift, but I felt pleased all the same by his generosity.

Next Queequeg solemnly divided his money into two equal piles and presented me with one, as a sign of our new friendship.

Later that night, in the same spirit of friendship, Queequeg invited me to take part in his pagan ceremony. Afterwards we talked and shared his pipe between us.

1. thine: Yours.
2. He had been a harpooner before becoming a priest.
3. In an Old Testament story, Jonah disobeyed God and was swallowed by a great fish before eventually being saved.

In his strange version of English he told me all about his home. I feel I now understand his story enough to retell it here.

Queequeg was originally from an island called Kokovoko. His father was the High Chief of a tribe of cannibals. One day, a whaling ship visited their island.

Having a spirit of adventure about him, Queequeg wanted to see the world and begged the captain to let him join the crew.

The ship was full so he was refused. Did this rejection deter him? Not at all! He sailed his canoe out to meet the ship then climbed up and onto the deck.

The captain was astonished and threatened to throw Queequeg overboard if he didn't return to his island.

But brave Queequeg grabbed hold of a ring and grasped it tightly, ignoring all the captain's threats.

The captain even threatened to cut Queequeg's hands off with a cutlass, but to no effect. So eventually the captain was forced to allow him to join the crew.

Queequeg and I now discussed our future plans and decided to join the same whaling ship. We would share any excitement and adventures that came our way.

NANTUCKET

It was late when we reached Nantucket, and needing somewhere to spend the night, we found ourselves at The Try Pots Inn.[1] I thought that the two pots hanging outside looked eerily like a gallows awaiting doomed men.

The inn was owned by Hosea Hussey and his wife. They served a choice of fish chowders for breakfast, lunch and dinner.[2] Hungry from our journey, we happily set about our meal.

Next morning I left Queequeg and Yojo, his idol, to a day of fasting while I went to find us a ship. Queequeg said Yojo foretold that I alone must select our vessel.

I soon heard of three vessels preparing for three-year voyages. Having looked at each in turn, I decided on the *Pequod*.

The ship itself was old-fashioned and rather small. Then I met one of the owners: old Captain Peleg.

Want to see what whaling is, eh? Have ye clapped eye on Captain Ahab?

I told him I wished to learn whaling and to see the world. He told me that Ahab was the present captain, whose leg had been eaten by a monstrous whale.

What dost thou think of him, Bildad?

He'll do.

The other owner, Captain Bildad then appeared. He and Peleg almost came to blows over what lay I should receive.[3]

Blast ye, Captain Bildad!

1. try-pots: Pots in which whale blubber is boiled to extract the oil.
2. chowder: A thick, creamy soup often made with fish. It is often associated with New England.
3. lay: Share of the profits from a whaling vessel.

That evening . . .

Get the axe! For God's sake, run for the doctor, some one, while I pry it open!

Queequeg, what's the matter with you?

After knocking on Queequeg's door several times without answer, I began to worry. The door was locked from inside!

Mrs Hussey and I were both quite sure Queequeg was dead. I burst through the door expecting the worst, but found him sitting calmly on the floor with Yojo on his head.

He's not been baptised right, or it would have washed some of that devil's blue off his face.[1]

You see him small drop of tar dere? Well spose him one whale eye.

After breakfast, we made our way to the *Pequod*. Captain Peleg announced that he let no cannibal onboard unless they proved that they had converted to Christianity.

I did my best to reassure him. Satisfied, Peleg invited Queequeg onboard and asked if he'd ever struck a fish.

Immediately, Queequeg jumped up and aimed his harpoon at a point on the dock.

We must have Hedgehog there, I mean Quohog, in one of our boats.

He darted the harpoon and struck the very same spot of glistening tar he'd pointed to! Peleg and Bildad were awestruck, and almost fell over each other to get the ship's papers for Queequeg to sign.

Realising the benefits of such an exact harpooner, Peleg asked him to sign, but seemed to stumble over Queequeg's name.

Queequeg took the offered quill, and made a strange figure on the paper; a symbol I later learned meant 'infinity'.[2]

1. devil's blue: Queequeg's tattoos.
2. quill: A bird's feather made into a pen for writing.

Setting Sail

We had just left the ship and were strolling along peacefully when a stranger stopped to ask if we had shipped in the *Pequod*.[1] He was shabbily dressed and had only one arm. He seemed very strange.

Deciding he must be mad, we tried to leave. But the stranger called us back and asked if we had met Captain Ahab. The man said his name was Elijah, which I hoped was not an ill omen.[2]

For several days there was great activity aboard as the *Pequod* was prepared. The sails were mended and supplies for the long voyage were brought on board.

Dawn next day was grey and misty as Queequeg and I went to the docks. We saw the mysterious Elijah again, and once more his strange words unsettled me, as they seemed to make no sense.

We finally boarded the *Pequod* where everything seemed to be quiet. My encounter with Elijah must have affected me, as once or twice I thought I saw shadows moving just out of sight. I tried to shake off a feeling of uneasiness.

1. shipped: Joined the crew.
2. Elijah: The name of an Old Testament prophet who foretold the death of the evil King Ahab.

Perry dood seat. My country way, won't hurt him face.

Suddenly we came across a man face down, and sound asleep. As he seemed to be the only other soul onboard, I suggested we sit and wait. So without further ado, Queequeg prodded the man and sat down upon his back!

Queequeg told me that as there were no sofas in his native land, his father the king would often fatten his servants to make them more comfortable to sit on.

Holloa, who be ye smokers?

The Captain came aboard last night.

God bless ye, and have ye in His holy keeping, men.

I told Queequeg to get off, which he did. Then he lit his pipe and we shared it. The sleeper awoke and I told him that we were part of the crew.

Later, amongst all the hustle and bustle, I saw old Captain Bildad pacing the deck, reluctant to go.

Eventually Captains Bildad and Peleg clambered into their small boat to return to shore, and our voyage finally got underway.

A cold, damp breeze was blowing and with a chorus of cheering, we set sail into the lonely Atlantic.

It seemed odd that Captain Ahab should stay unseen in his cabin – but he did. We saw no sign of him for several days.

CAPTAIN AHAB

Captain Ahab was tall and broad-shouldered, and in place of the leg he'd lost was an ivory leg, carved from the jaw of a sperm whale.

Ahab slotted his leg into holes in the deck to stop himself from slipping.

If ye see a white one, split your lungs for him![1]

Next morning, Stubb advised Flask not to speak harshly to Ahab, no matter what. He then warned him to look out for a white whale.

For lunch, we gathered around the crew's table and Dough-Boy the steward served us. Daggoo was forced to sit on the floor as he was too tall to sit at table!

Come here, so we may pick your bones clean!

Dough-Boy was nervous serving the cannibals, Queequeg and Tashtego. They teased and jabbed at him mercilessly.

Skin your eyes for him, men; look sharp for white water.[2]

One morning after breakfast, Ahab nailed a gold doubloon to the mast. It was for the first man to catch a white whale with a wrinkled brow and a crooked jaw.

That white whale must be the same that some call Moby Dick.

Ahab confirmed that the white whale was indeed Moby Dick. The first mate, Starbuck, then asked if it was Moby Dick who took Ahab's leg. Ahab confirmed it, swearing to get his revenge.

Starbuck called Ahab's obsession with the whale madness. But Ahab, filled with a passion, ordered the harpooners to remove the barbed, iron ends from their poles and fill them with liquor.

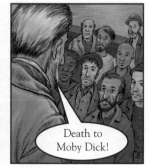

Death to Moby Dick!

He ordered the harpooners to drink, and swear an oath to kill Moby Dick. Turning to the rest of the crew, he called upon us to do the same.

54

1. split your lungs: Shout as loudly as possible.
2. white water: A sign that a whale is present.

I now prophesy that I will dismember my dismemberer.[1]

Captain Ahab retired to his cabin. He knew the crew thought him mad, but he swore to kill the whale no matter what.

How big is this creature?

I had shouted my oath along with the rest of the crew, and yet I knew nothing of the whale. Wild rumours circulated amongst the men, who told me how Ahab had come to lose his leg.

He fought the white whale single-handedly.

Surrounded by the wrecks of three boats, and with his men and oars stranded, Ahab had battled the whale.

He seized a large knife and bravely lunged forward, trying to stab Moby Dick to death.

But as the whale's sickle-shaped jaw swept by, it severed Ahab's leg like a mower cutting grass.

In his pain and fury, Ahab had raved about the white whale, blaming him for all the evils in the world. Gripped by madness, the captain was secured in a strait-jacket by the crew. [2]

After some time, Ahab took over the ship again and began to issue orders once more. But the madness still lurked beneath the surface.

In his cabin onboard the *Pequod*, Ahab studied his large sea charts. He had chosen to set sail earlier in the year than normal so that he could spend extra time hunting Moby Dick.

1. dismember: Remove part of the whale that took his leg.
2. strait-jacket: A jacket with very long sleeves used to restrain violent movement.

"There She Blows!"

It was a warm, lazy afternoon and Queequeg and I were weaving a sword-mat, when I heard Tashtego shout out in excitement.[1] It was our first sighting of whales!

Immediately, the crew sprang into action. Tashtego scrambled down from watch and Ahab quickly ordered the crew to the boats.

Suddenly, five strangers appeared seemingly from thin air! These men were Ahab's personal boat crew, their existence kept secret from the rest of us, who stared in amazement at the strangers.

Ahab ignored our surprise though and ordered the boats lowered.

One of these strangers, Fedallah, seemed to be their leader. He oversaw the others cast loose the tackles and set off.

Three more boats took to the water and followed Ahab's craft. I took my place in the final boat, led by Starbuck, with Queequeg as our harpooner.

Without warning, a mist descended and the sea became rough, making it difficult to see.

In another boat, Flask climbed onto the giant Daggoo's shoulders to try to see into the distance.

1. sword-mat: A tightly woven mat.

The wind was fierce and we were swept along at maddening speeds. The whales seemed all around, and our boats split up to chase them.

At last, a whale surfaced near us. Fearless Queequeg seized his chance and threw his harpoon.

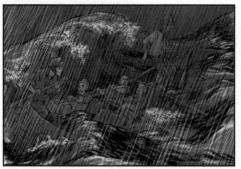

There she breaches! The white whale, the white whale!

Waves swamped the boat and we were tossed out into the squall.[1] But the whale, only grazed by Queequeg's iron, escaped and we clambered back into the boat, wet and cold.

One morning, Daggoo saw a white shape in the distance. He saw it rise and fall several times, and excitedly called out that he saw Moby Dick. Soon the small boats were in pursuit.

However, as we drew nearer I saw that it was not Moby Dick but a giant squid, its long tentacles trailing in the water. The squid seemed like a ghost, and with a sucking sound, sank beneath the waves.

The great live squid, which they say, few whaleships beheld and returned to their ports to tell of it.

The squid had a strange effect on Starbuck who gazed at the spot where it had disappeared for some time. He said he almost wished he'd seen Moby Dick instead.

1. squall: Storm.

STUBB'S SUPPER

Queequeg also thought the great squid was a sign, but he thought it meant sperm whales were nearby.

On my watch, I saw a gigantic sperm whale break the surface, the sun shining on his broad back. I instantly called out.

Ahab ordered the boats out and the crew erupted in excited shouts. The noise alarmed the whale and it turned to swim away. Ahab ordered us to speak only in whispers and so we paddled after our prey in silence.

As the whale surfaced Stubb struck at it, turning the sea red. Finally, it blew out a spout of blood-tinged water and died.

The whale had been killed some distance from the *Pequod*, so three of the boats began to drag it back. My arms were fit to drop off by the time we arrived with our cargo.

To my surprise, Ahab seemed indifferent² to our catch, as if it reminded him that Moby Dick still lived. He gave orders to secure the carcass to the side of the ship and then retired for the night.

Stubb loved whale steaks, and sent Daggoo to cut him one. By the time Stubb sat down to his strange supper it was almost midnight.

The terrible noise of hungry sharks tearing at the whale carcass, and the slap of their tails against the hull, was surely enough to terrify the sleepers down below deck.

1. both pipes smoked out: Stubb's pipe burned out at the same time that the whale died.
2. indifferent: Uninterested.

Stubb liked to joke and asked the cook, Fleece, to tell the sharks to be quiet as he could hardly think.

We took turns to drive the sharks away – or they would soon eat the whole whale. We killed some, and the sea was soon a frenzy of sharks feeding on each other.

Queequeg pulled a shark onto deck to skin it, but the shark was not dead and almost bit poor Queequeg's hand off!

We set to work removing the blubber from the whale's carcass. Once a strip of blubber is freed, the whale is peeled in sections, much like peeling an orange. The huge, white remains of the whale were then cut adrift, and were set upon almost immediately by sharks and dozens of screaming seabirds.

ANGELS AND DEVILS

After several days, another whaling-ship was spotted in the distance – the *Jeroboam* from Nantucket. It lowered a boat which soon drew alongside the *Pequod*.

The *Jeroboam*'s Captain Mayhew said there was a contagious epidemic onboard and he was fearful of infecting us.[1]

That's he! that's he!

Stubb recognised the other man as one who had claimed to be a great prophet before joining the *Jeroboam*.

This man had said that he was the Archangel Gabriel, and promptly ordered the captain to jump overboard. He was now so powerful the captain had to keep him aboard.

Ahab told Mayhew that he did not fear their epidemic and invited him aboard, but Gabriel objected. All Ahab was interested in was news of Moby Dick though, and he began to question the two sailors.

Hast thou seen the white whale?

The conversation was difficult as the waves kept pushing the small boat away. Mayhew and Gabriel had to keep rowing back.

Macey disappeared!

Mayhew told a bleak tale about Moby Dick. A former crewman named Macey, was killed when the whale tossed him from his boat, never to be seen again.

1. epidemic: An infectious disease that is widespread in a particular area.

Beware the blasphemer's end!

Gabriel claimed this death was an omen. He had warned against pursuing Moby Dick, but Macey wouldn't listen, and so had died.

Ahab remembered a letter onboard for the *Jeroboam* and tried to pass it over. It was for Macey.

Keep it thyself, thou art soon going that way.

But Gabriel grabbed the letter and piercing it with a knife, threw both to land at Ahab's feet. Then the *Jeroboam*'s small boat sped away.

I wonder what the old man wants with this lump of foul lard.

This episode over, life returned to normal. After several days, Ahab spotted a right whale and sent Stubb and Flask to catch it. Right whales were thought inferior catches, so the men were confused at Ahab's orders.[1]

It is Fedallah's advice.

Flask explained that he'd heard Fedallah say that a ship with a sperm whale's head on one side, and a right whale's head on the other would never capsize.

He's the devil, I say.

He wondered why Ahab had anything to do with Fedallah. Stubb then said he believed Ahab had sold his soul to him to catch Moby Dick.

1. right whales: Slow-moving whales that were hunted for their blubber.

A Lucky Escape

The sperm whale's head lashed to one side caused the *Pequod* to list severely. By adding the right whale's head, we soon regained our balance.

Tashtego climbed onto the sperm whale to 'tap the tun'.[1] He carefully cut a hole and began collecting the valuable whale oil in a bucket.

Suddenly, Tashtego slipped and disappeared head-first into the hole!

Aaagh!

Man overboard!

Daggoo tried to pass a bucket down so Tashtego could climb out. But his extra weight sent the whale's head crashing into the sea where it immediately began to sink.

We heard another loud splash as brave Queequeg, sword in hand, dived in to rescue Tashtego. We rushed to the side of the ship eager for signs of life.

Soon Daggoo shouted that he saw them. Queequeg had dived under the whale's head, cut a hole in the bottom and then dragged Tashtego out by his long hair.

Later we encountered a German whaling vessel called the *Jungfrau*. They seemed eager to speak with us and sent across their captain, Derick De Beer.

1. tun: Removing the oil from the whale's head. A tun is also the name of a barrel or cask for wine or beer.

De Beer came begging for lamp oil and Ahab was so eager for news of Moby Dick that he let him aboard. But De Beer knew nothing.

As De Beer headed back to the *Jungfrau,* a pod of whales was spotted.[1] We saw an old bull whale swimming much slower than the others, and as we drew closer, we saw that this ancient creature only had one fin.

Better luck next time!

Sure of his crew's triumph, De Beer taunted us, much to Starbuck's fury. But unlucky for him, he nearly capsized and we took the lead.

Our harpooners leapt up and their barbs all struck the old whale. Our boats were pulled forward and we sailed right ahead of the Germans.

So it was, that the *Pequod* claimed the carcass of that crippled old whale.

Who darted that stone lance? And when? Was it before America was even discovered?

Under the whale's skin we found a corroded harpoon from a previous hunt. We also discovered a stone harpoon-head, with the wound long healed. That made me wonder at the age of this creature.

But our efforts to secure the whale ended in failure – the carcass seemed determined to sink. Finally, we were forced to cut the lines and release the body of the ancient whale, in case he dragged us down.

---

1. pod: The name for a group of whales.

The *Rose-Bud*

In time, we reached waters popular with sperm whales and Ahab's hope of finding Moby Dick grew. So desperate was he, that he opted not to stop to take on more fresh water.

We saw a continuous chain of whale-jets sparkling in the air. The crew crowded into the boats and we gave chase, driving the whales ahead of us.

When whales are plentiful, the aim is to kill as many as possible, or at least to injure them so that you may kill them at a later time.

To do this, we used druggs.[1] This extra weight made it much more difficult for harpooned whales to escape.

They are amazing creatures.

The cows and calves seemed fearless, and came right up to the boats like dogs. It was wonderful to watch these mighty creatures so closely, and in such peace.

We were spellbound by the whale nursery, disturbed only by the thrashing of the injured whales. But only one whale was captured that day, the rest escaped.

Another loss that day was Queequeg's hat which was knocked from his head and never seen again.

1. druggs: Blocks of wood that could be fastened to harpoons.

> It may contain something worth a good deal more than oil.

> What's the matter with your nose, broke it?

> I wish I didn't have any nose at all!

We came across a French ship, the *Rose-Bud,* with two whales strapped to the sides. The stench was disgusting, and Stubb wondered if one of the whales contained ambergris.[1]

Stubb decided to try and trick the French crew into abandoning their whales. Holding his nose, he called out to a French crewman. This man was not happy with the stench, so Stubb used him to trick their captain.

> As we value our lives – cut loose from these fish.

> If you get the captain, I'll save you from this dirty scrape.[2]

The crew kept climbing up the masts for fresher air. Using the crewman to translate, Stubb told the captain that the whales carried a fever which would kill the crew. Terrified, the inexperienced captain ordered the carcasses cut free.

> I have it, I have it!

Generous Stubb offered to help by towing one carcass away himself. He was pleased to have secured the possible source of valuable ambergris for the *Pequod*.

Thrusting his hands into the whale, he pulled out something that appeared to be ripe old cheese, but it was worth a fortune!

As Ahab often paced the quarter-deck he gazed at his doubloon. He announced his intention that the white whale be raised from the sea within a month and a day.

---

1. ambergris: A foul-smelling, waxy substance produced by some sperm whales. It was very valuable and used in perfume manufacture.
2. If the French crewman helps Stubb, he won't have to continue working with the stinking dead whales.

NEWS OF THE WHITE WHALE

"Hast seen the White Whale?"

Now in popular whaling waters, we saw an English whaler, the *Samuel Enderby*. Ahab hailed them, hoping for news of Moby Dick.

"I was ignorant of the White Whale at that time . . ."

Captain Boomer said that indeed they saw the white whale last season, and that it cost him his arm.

While trying to catch a harpooned whale, a huge whale with a wrinkled white head had appeared. It tried to bite through the harpoon line, but became tangled in it.

Boomer's boat had then attacked Moby Dick, but he thrashed about, bringing the line down across the boat and slicing it in two.[1] The crew were pitched into the sea.

Boomer tried to grab hold of the iron – harpoons from Ahab's previous attack – stuck in the whale's side.

Then, tragedy! Another harpoon flew forward and pierced Boomer's arm. He was pinned to the whale and thought he would drown. But then luckily it came free.

At this point the ship's doctor took over the story. For days Boomer's wound grew worse, until the doctor was forced to remove his arm. But Ahab didn't care, he just wanted to know more about Moby Dick.

"This man's blood, it's at the boiling point! His pulse makes these planks beat!"

Boomer confessed they had seen the whale twice since then, but feeling that the loss of one arm was enough, didn't give chase. Dr Bunger warned Ahab that Moby Dick was best left alone but realised that Ahab was obsessed with it.

Ahab didn't care for the warning either, and learning that the white whale had headed east, called his crew back to the boat, and we returned to the *Pequod*.

1. line: The rope attached to the harpoons.

Let it leak! I'm all aleak myself. Aye! Leaks in leaks!

The next morning . . .

Starbuck reported that the casks were leaking, and we could lose more whale oil in an hour, than we could catch in a year.

There is one God that is Lord over the earth, and one Captain that is lord over the *Pequod*.

Starbuck argued, but Ahab ordered him to leave his cabin, pointing a loaded musket at him. Starbuck told Ahab that his greatest threat came from Ahab himself.

In the midst of this, my friend Queequeg had come down with a fever, and each day seemed closer to death. He wasted away, becoming thinner and thinner.

Queequeg said he'd like to be buried in a canoe, as was his island's custom. The carpenter was called for to make Queequeg's coffin – the closest we could get to a canoe.

Queequeg climbed into his coffin with his harpoon and little wooden idol, but slowly he seemed to rally and returned to health.

He later said that if a man made up his mind to live, mere sickness couldn't kill him. The coffin was not wasted though, as Queequeg used it as a sea chest.

For the white fiend!

Ahab asked Perth, the blacksmith if he could make a special harpoon to kill Moby Dick. Perth made many different blades, until finally the old man was satisfied.

Ahab said the harpoon must be tempered with the blood of the harpooners, Queequeg, Tashtego and Daggoo.[1] They each cut their arms, letting the blood flow onto the barb.

Ego non baptizo te in nomine patris, sed in nomine diaboli![2]

Ahab seemed crazed at this point, and as the blood touched the iron, he howled out what was both a prayer and a curse over this strange baptism.

1. tempered: Improve the hardness or flexibility of metal by heating it and adding substances to it.
2. This is Latin for: I baptise you not in the name of the father, but in the name of the devil!

THE PROPHECY

I have dreamed it again.

Have I not said, old man, that neither hearse nor coffin can be thine?

We then caught and killed four whales, but one was so far from the *Pequod* that Ahab's small boat had to stay with it to prevent it being stolen or eaten.

Fedallah watched the sharks circling the carcass. Ahab awoke, and reported dreams about hearses and coffins.

Then Fedallah made an incredible prophecy to Captain Ahab.[1]

. . . wood of the last one must be grown in America.

I shall still go before thee thy pilot.

I am immortal then, on land and on sea.

Fedallah said that Ahab must see two hearses before he could die – the first not made by mortal hands, and the second made of wood from America.

Fedallah also said he would die first, but reappear later as a guide. At first, Ahab was amused.

Finally Fedallah told Ahab that only hemp could kill him, which Ahab took to mean the gallows.[2] Sure nothing could kill him, he laughed.

Oh! Jolly is the gale, And a joker is the whale, A'flourishin' his tale...

Sailing in tropical waters meant fearsome storms were common and, sure enough, one night the *Pequod* was caught in a typhoon. The main sails tore and the ship was tossed about in the huge waves, but Stubb calmly sang a song.

1. prophecy: Predicting events that are yet to occur.
2: hemp: Plant fibres used to make rope.

> Look aloft!
> The corpusants![1]

Lightning flashed, thunder crashed and Ahab felt the storm was leading him to the white whale. Suddenly, Starbuck called out for us to look up at the yard-arms. To my amazement, the three main masts were all tipped with ghostly flames!

The scar on Ahab's face had been caused by lightning and he seemed to pray to the spirit of the flames. Suddenly his harpoon was hit by lightning and flames erupted.

Terrified by this show of strength by nature, some of the crew began to talk of mutiny.

> All your oaths to hunt the white whale are as binding as mine.

Hearing this, Ahab raised his still burning harpoon, and waving it amongst his mutinous and wretched crew, he threatened to impale the first man to leave his post.

The crew fell back, and fiery Ahab reminded them of the oath they all swore to kill Moby Dick. This said, Ahab put out the flame and plunged us into darkness.

---

1. corpusants: Balls of light sometimes seen about the masts of ships during a storm, possibly ball lightning.

AFTER THE STORM

After midnight, the typhoon finally grew calm. In such a storm it was common for the compass needles to spin, making it impossible to steer accurately.

> Shall this crazed old man be suffered to drag a whole ship's company to doom with him?

Starbuck entered Ahab's room to tell him this, and saw a pair of loaded muskets in a rack upon the wall.

> A touch, and Starbuck may survive to hug his wife and child again.

Taking a musket in his shaking hand, Starbuck walked towards Ahab's hammock. He remembered Ahab's oath and his threats to the crew.

> Oh, Moby Dick, I clutch thy heart at last.

Ahab stirred restlessly, dreaming of the whale, and Starbuck realised he could not murder him.

After steadying his hand, Starbuck replaced the musket and returned to deck with a heavy heart.

> Thou liest!

> East-sou-east, sir.

The next morning, as Ahab silently watched the rising sun, he suddenly hurried towards the helm and asked in which direction the ship was heading.

We were heading in the wrong direction! By the position of the sun, Ahab realised that the compass needles had been inverted by the storm.[1]

> Out of this bit of steel Ahab can make one of his own that will point as true as any.

He immediately changed course and asked for a sailmaker's needle and an old lance. It was thought bad luck by sailors to sail using inverted needles, so Ahab made a new compass.

> The sun is East, and that compass swears it!

1. inverted: Opposite to the normal position.

> Those are the voices of newly drowned men in the sea.

Near the Equator, we passed a cluster of rocky islets from which came an unearthly sound. Some said it was mermaids, but the Manxman, the oldest sailor onboard, said they were ghostly voices.[1]

These islets were also popular with seals – another bad omen. This added to the uneasiness on the voyage.

> Aaaarrgggh!

The tension grew again when early one morning, an unfortunate sailor climbed the mast, lost his hold and fell into the sea.

A life-buoy was quickly thrown in after him. I wondered if perhaps the sailor was still half-asleep when he climbed the mast.

But it was no use. The life-buoy, dried out by the hot sun, filled with water and soon followed the sailor to the bottom of the sea.

This crew were nervous and now quite sure that evil signs were warning them against the pursuit of the white whale. The lost life-buoy needed to be replaced so Queequeg offered his coffin to be made into a new one.

---

1. Manxman: Someone from the Isle of Man.

LOST AT SEA

Next morning a fast-moving ship, the *Rachel*, drew alongside and hailed us. Ahab immediately asked if they had seen Moby Dick, and Captain Gardiner said yes.

He asked us to help find his missing whale-boat. Stubb was sceptical about why we should help, and voiced his suspicions.[1]

The day before, Gardiner's ship had seen Moby Dick. Most of the boats were already miles away, so the last was lowered with his son onboard, and had not been seen since.

Gardiner begged to charter the *Pequod* for two days to search for his son's boat.[2] He appealed to Ahab to take pity and help him, but Ahab hard-heartedly refused.

Shocked by Ahab's refusal, the crew's good humour vanished. Convinced that he wouldn't be told if Moby Dick was sighted, Ahab had Starbuck hoist him up the main mast.

From this viewpoint, Ahab could see for miles around. He gazed so intently at the horizon for a sign of Moby's spout, that he failed to see a seahawk approaching him.

The hawk came closer, and grabbed Ahab's hat in its sharp, curved talons, and flew off.

Ahab's hat was gone! We saw a black spot falling from a great height as the bird finally dropped it.

1. sceptical: Suspicious and disbelieving.
2. charter: Hiring a boat.

Hast seen the white whale? Hast killed him?

The harpoon is not yet forged that ever will do that.

The mood onboard did not improve as we sailed on. Soon, we came upon a ship miserably misnamed the *Delight*. On its side was the shattered remains of a whale-boat.

Assuming that the damage was caused by Moby Dick, Ahab feverishly asked the captain for news.

The captain confirmed both that Moby Dick was responsible . . . and that he still lived.

Tempered in blood, and tempered by lightning are these barbs.

Are ye ready there?

Hearing this, Ahab grabbed Perth's harpoon, and showed it to the *Delight*'s captain. He promised that this was the one to kill Moby Dick.

The captain wished Ahab luck and returned to the funeral of one of the men killed by Moby Dick – the only body they managed to recover.

As we left, we heard a splash as the dead man, sewn inside his hammock, hit the sea.

Forty years of continual whaling! Forty years on the pitiless sea!

My captain! Let us fly these deadly waters! Let us home!

Is Ahab, Ahab? Is it I, God, or who, that lifts this arm?

Starbuck sensed a deep sadness in his captain, as Ahab remembered the day he struck his first whale when he was just 18 years old. He confessed that of the past 40 years, he had spent most at sea.

Ahab admitted that his wife became a widow soon after they were wed. When he questioned his pursuit of Moby Dick, Starbuck begged him to turn back.

But Starbuck's hopes were dashed once and for all, as Ahab spoke passionately about being commanded beyond his power to chase the white whale to the ends of the earth.

THE CHASE

There she blows! A hump like a snow-hill! It is Moby Dick!

That same night, Ahab ordered the crew to prepare for the chase. He felt certain that Moby Dick was near, and was desperate to be ready.

Ahab was being hoisted up the mast when he let out a terrific cry. In an instant, the other lookouts shouted . . . it was Moby Dick!

Ahab thought it was a good omen that he spotted the whale, and therefore kept the doubloon himself.

Led by Ahab, three boats set off in the direction of the whale's last spout. Fedallah's eyes seemed oddly bright, and he chewed at his lips.

Boats! Boats!

A flock of birds around Ahab's boat alerted him to the whale below them. As he peered down into the water he saw a tiny white spot in the deep, but growing larger by the second.

He tried desperately to steer out of the way as Moby Dick broke the surface, mouth gaping. The boat was bitten in half! Ahab was tipped into the sea, while the whale lashed the waves higher with his tail.

Moby Dick seemed to be swimming in circles, trying to create a whirlpool. Ahab narrowly escaped, and swam to Stubb's boat where he lay panting.

Ahab rubbed his bloodshot eyes and his first question was not about his crew, but his harpoon.

Assured that both his harpoon and his crew were safe, Ahab made haste back towards the safety of the *Pequod*.

Back onboard, Ahab assumed a state of readiness; alert and scanning the waves for a sign of Moby Dick. Seeing nothing, he went to examine the wreck of the whale-boat.

Starbuck warned him that losing any whale-boat was unlucky, but as it was the captain's own boat it was a particularly bad omen.

Ahab, however, dismissed these concerns as nonsense. He ordered Starbuck to resume the search for Moby Dick, but to be careful not to attack during the night.

MOBY DICK

At dawn . . .

The next morning, we spotted Moby Dick, still trailing the harpoons of other long-gone crews, as well as Ahab's. The boats were lowered and the chase began.

The boats were moving fast, but instead of fleeing, Moby Dick turned and swam towards them. Ahab cheered his men on, saying he would take the whale head-on, but almost immediately the whale charged!

The huge white whale seemed not to notice the many harpoons that stabbe and tore into his flesh.

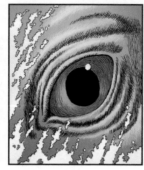

Aaargh!

He seemed to focus on the total destruction of each of the whale-boats and the men within them.

Although wounded, the diabolic creature cunningly used the lines to tangle and smash the boats against one another.

1. diabolic: Evil

Ahab's boat was flipped over the whale's head, tipping men into the sea. Victoriously, Moby Dick swam lazily away, trailing lines behind him. Ahab swam back to the *Pequod*.

All eyes fell on Ahab, whose ivory leg had snapped off.

It was soon noticed that Fedallah was missing. Stubb said that he had become tangled in Ahab's line and was dragged down below the waves.

Ahab remembered Fedallah's prophecy that he would die first. It then seemed to Ahab that it was his destiny to continue on his quest.

The mood on the *Pequod* was solemn. The next day would be crucial, so work continued sharpening harpoons. The sound of hammering lasted through the night.

In the meantime, Perth the carpenter set to work making another leg for Ahab. In the distance, Moby Dick remained in sight until the sun set.

A Prophecy Fulfilled

Dawn broke on another fair day, although the crew were still tense with anticipation. At last Ahab saw the spout, and instantly the three lookouts called out, too.

As the whale-boats descended, Ahab looked around and called Starbuck to him. Ahab offered his hand, and Starbuck, touched by the old man's nobility, begged him again not to go. But Ahab could not be persuaded.

As the boats pulled away, Starbuck called out – Ahab's boat was ringed by sharks! Ignoring the other boats, the sharks surrounded Ahab's, but the old man did not hear the warning.

Moby Dick rose up from the sea and we saw the irons from yesterday's attack dotted over his huge body.[1] A shout went up and there, caught in the lines that trailed from the whale, was the body of Fedallah.

Astonished, the harpoon fell from Ahab's hand as he remembered the prophecy: "I will reappear to guide you." Then he ordered us to get ready to attack.

Ahab's boat came alongside the whale and he stabbed his harpoon deep into Moby Dick's side. Thrashing around in pain, the whale managed to sink Ahab's boat for a third time before heading for the *Pequod*.

1. irons: Harpoons.

Dash on, my men!

Curse you, Moby Dick!

Ahab joined another boat and urged us to quickly return to the ship. But it was too late.

The whale smashed into the side of the *Pequod* and water flooded in. As it began to sink, Ahab realised his own ship was the second hearse of Fedallah's prophecy. He made a final, desperate stab at Moby Dick.

"Only hemp can kill thee!"

Bending over to clear the harpoon's line, a flying rope caught Ahab around the neck and, in an instant, he was gone.

For a moment we stood in shocked silence, watching the *Pequod* sinking fast. The hull was already beneath the waves.

Suddenly the pull of the sinking ship began to drag at the boats and they started to spin. This vortex soon pulled the boats, oars and all the men downwards, and out of sight.[1] Fate chose to save me alone.

I watched this scene of horror while clinging onto Queequeg's coffin. I stayed like this for a day and a night until the *Rachel*, still searching for her missing children, found another orphan.

THE END

1. vortex: A whirling or spiralling movement of water.

Robinson Crusoe

Daniel Defoe

Illustrated by

Penko Gelev

Retold by

Ian Graham

Series created and designed by

David Salariya

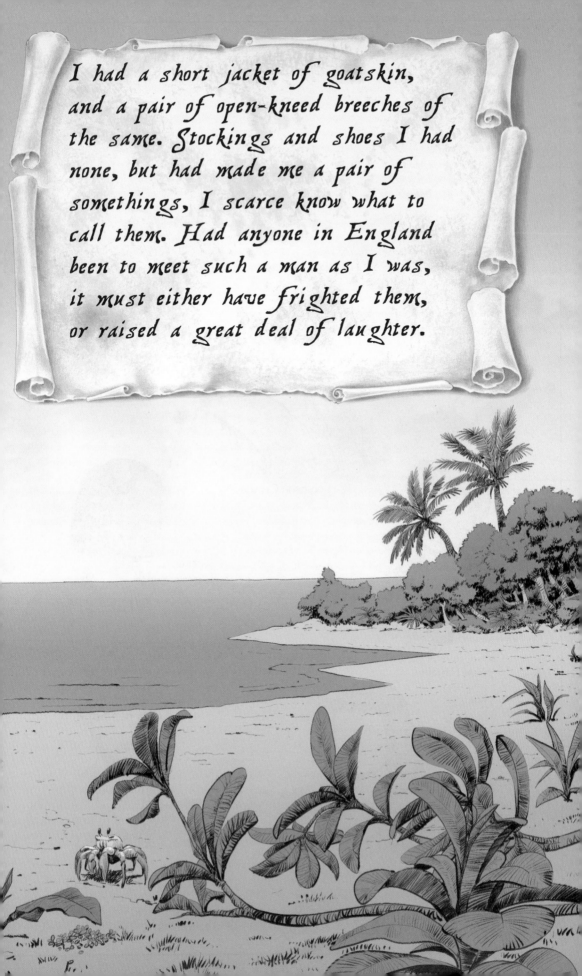

I had a short jacket of goatskin, and a pair of open-kneed breeches of the same. Stockings and shoes I had none, but had made me a pair of somethings, I scarce know what to call them. Had anyone in England been to meet such a man as I was, it must either have frighted them, or raised a great deal of laughter.

CHARACTERS

Robinson's mother

Robinson's father

Robinson Crusoe

Xury, a slave of the
pirate captain

Friday

A plantation owner
in Brazil

A Moroccan
pirate captain

THE CALL OF THE SEA

York, England

Robinson Crusoe was born here in 1632.

My name is Robinson Crusoe.

His oldest brother, a soldier, died fighting the Spanish.

Nobody knows what became of his second brother.

Robinson's father wants his son to be a lawyer, but Robinson has other ideas.

I will be satisfied with nothing but going to sea!

His father asks him why he is so determined to leave home.

What reasons more than a mere wandering inclination[1] do you have for leaving your father's house?

When his father becomes upset, Robinson at first agrees to stay at home…

My heart is so full[2] I can say no more.

…but his dream will not leave him.

He tells his mother that his mind is made up.

I am resolved[3] to run away and see the world.

1. a mere wandering inclination: an idle wish to travel.
2. My heart is so full: I am experiencing such strong feelings (in this case, sadness).
3. I am resolved: I have decided.

Leaving Home

Robinson meets a friend while visiting the port of Hull.

I'm going by sea to London in my father's ship.

He has finally got his chance to go to sea!

1 September 1651

Robinson Crusoe boards a ship for the first time.

As the wind tosses the ship about, he becomes terribly seasick and fears for his life.

Please, God, if you will spare my life on this one voyage, I will go directly home.

His friend teases him.

You were frighted[1] when it blew a capful of wind.[2]

Feeling better, he forgets his vow to return home.

The ship is soon forced to shelter from another storm.

Strike the topmasts![3]

The wind increases. Even the captain fears for their fate.

Lord be merciful to us! We shall all be lost![4]

86   1. frighted: frightened.   2. a capful of wind: a light breeze.   3. Strike the topmasts: Lower the top section of each mast (to reduce the ship's wind resistance).   4. We shall all be lost: We will all die.

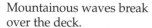

Mountainous waves break over the deck.

The crew cut down the masts to save the ship.

She's going to founder![1]

Lord save us!

We have sprung a leak.

There is four foot[2] of water in the hold.[3]

The captain orders guns to be fired to signal for help.

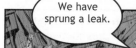

BOOM!!

FIRE!

A boat arrives just in time.

She's sinking!

Just 15 minutes later, they see their ship disappear beneath the waves.

I should be laughed at were I to return to my home in such a miserable state.

My thanks to you for such great humanity.[4]

Robinson and the other sailors are given food and lodging by their rescuers.

Robinson decides that he can't go home a failure, so he must press on to London and go back to sea.

1. founder: sink.   2. four foot: 1.2 metres.
3. hold: the part of a ship where the cargo is stored.   4. humanity: kindness.

Voyage into Slavery

In London, a ship's captain invites Robinson on his next voyage to Africa. Robinson jumps at the chance.

If you would go the voyage with me as my messmate[1] and companion...

...there will be no expense.

The captain schools Robinson in the arts of navigation.[2]

The heat near the equator[3] gives Robinson a fever.

But he recovers to become a successful trader, returning to London a wealthy man.

Now I am a sailor *and* set up as a Guinea[4] trader.

The captain falls ill during the voyage and dies soon after his return to England.

Farewell, friend.

Ashes to ashes, dust to dust...

The new commander of the captain's ship invites Robinson to return to Africa with him.

Shall we voyage together?

Ay, sir.

Will you keep this safe for me?

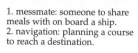

Robinson leaves most of his fortune with the captain's widow for safe-keeping.

Off the coast of West Africa...

I see a Sallee rover![5]

...a pirate ship looms out of a grey morning.

1. messmate: someone to share meals with on board a ship.
2. navigation: planning a course to reach a destination.

3. equator: an imaginary line around the middle of the Earth.   4. Guinea: a common name for Africa in the 17th century; nowadays, Guinea is a republic in western Africa.   5. Sallee rover: a pirate ship from the port of Salé in Morocco.

Robinson and the rest of the crew lie in wait for the pirates.

The guns thunder, sending cannonballs smashing into the pirate ship.

FIRE!

Fight for your lives!

Sixty pirates board the ship and start slashing the sails and rigging.[1]

Enough! With three men killed and eight wounded, we are obliged to yield.[2]

The crew have no chance of winning, so they surrender.

Robinson and the crew are taken as slaves to the Moroccan port of Salé.

You shall be my proper[3] prize, my slave.

The pirate captain claims Robinson as his personal slave.

My father was right — he said I should be miserable, with none to relieve[4] me, if I went to sea.

He is put to work cleaning the pirate captain's house.

1. rigging: the ropes and chains that hold up a ship's masts and control the sails.
2. obliged to yield: forced to surrender.   3. my proper: my own.   4. relieve: rescue.

A BID FOR FREEDOM

After two years, the pirate captain starts taking Robinson fishing with him.

Ready the pinnace![1]

One day the captain sends Robinson fishing without him.

A Moor[2] called Ishmael and a slave called Xury go with him.

Robinson secretly loads extra supplies.

He tricks Ishmael into bringing gunpowder and lead shot.

I shall bring powder and shot.

We may shoot some alcamies.[3]

They sail a mile offshore and start fishing.

Robinson suddenly grabs Ishmael around the waist...

Aarrgghh!

...and tosses him into the sea.

I beg you, take me into the boat. Don't leave me here to drown.

You swim well enough to reach to the shore.

If you will be faithful to me, I'll make you a great man.

Xury is afraid he might be thrown overboard too, but Robinson trusts him.

90

1. pinnace: a small boat with sails and oars for travelling between a ship and the shore.
2. Moor: a Muslim from North Africa.   3. alcamies: small brown shore birds with long, curved bills.

After five days' sailing, they anchor in the mouth of a river.

ROAR

HOOT

BARK

HOWL

The night is full of animal noises from the forest.

Let us weigh anchor[1] and row away.

No!

BLAM!

Robinson fires into the water to frighten off a beast they hear approaching the boat.

In the morning they wade ashore.

Robinson keeps watch while Xury searches for drinking water.

We will eat well tonight.

Xury shoots a hare-like animal for dinner.

They find fresh drinking water further upstream.

Dreadful monsters!

They sail along the coast, looking for an English ship that might take them home.

1. weigh anchor: raise the anchor.

RESCUE

Robinson recognises a group of islands and immediately knows where he is.

Those are the Cape de Verd Islands.[1]

Xury spots a ship and fears it might be the pirate captain coming to recapture them.

Master, master, a ship with a sail!

They are in luck: it's a Portuguese merchant ship.

A sailor on the ship spots their tiny boat in the distance.

They've seen us. They're shortening sail.[2]

It is some European boat!

The sailors question Robinson in various languages.

¿Quiénes sois?

Qui êtes-vous?

What are you?

I am an Englishman fleeing from slavery under the Moors in Sallee.

You may take everything I have in return for my deliverance.[3]

No, Seignor Inglese,[4] I will carry you thither in charity.[5]

The ship's captain refuses any payment for saving Robinson and taking him to Brazil.

When they arrive in Brazil, Xury decides to stay with the ship and work for the captain.

1. Cape de Verd Islands: the Cape Verde Islands, off the west coast of Africa.   2. shortening sail: furling (rolling up) some of their sails to make the ship slow down.   3. deliverance: rescue.   4. Seignor Inglese: Mister Englishman.
5. I will carry you thither in charity: I will take you there free of charge.

Robinson sells the captain a leopard skin and a lion skin.

He stays with the owner of a sugar plantation[1] and learns about the sugar business.

He buys some land and sets up his own plantation.

I live like a man cast away upon some desolate[2] island.

He feels lonely, working so hard that he rarely sees anyone else.

...and then the ship was struck by a monstrous wave.

At the port of St Salvadore[3] he amazes the merchants with his adventures.

Will you sail with our ship and bring back workers for our plantations?

Three merchants are sending a ship to Africa to buy slaves.[4]

Robinson accepts the offer. He makes a will[5] in case he does not return.

1 September 1659

Eight years to the day after he left his parents, Robinson boards another ship.

We will use these beads, shells and other trifles[6] for trading.

1. plantation: a large farm or estate where crops are grown to be sold. 2. desolate: bleak. 3. St Salvadore: now called Salvador da Bahia. It was the capital of colonial Brazil from 1549 to 1763. 4. slaves: Buying people in Africa to work as slaves in the Americas was common at this time; the slave trade was not banned until the 19th century. 5. will: a legal document setting out what is to happen to a person's money and possessions after his or her death. 6. trifles: worthless things.

93

SHIPWRECK!

At first the sea is calm and the weather is extremely hot.

A terrible storm overwhelms the ship. One sailor is washed into the sea.

Man overboard!

We should go directly back to Brazil.

No, we should make for the Carib-Islands.[1]

After the storm, Robinson persuades the captain to set course for the Caribbean.

But a second storm drives the ship westward, away from the Caribbean.

Land ahoy!

In the morning, the lookout spots land.

The ship hits a sandbar,[2] sending the crew flying.

There is no hope for the ship. The crew must take their chances in a small boat.

They row for the shore, fearing their boat will be smashed to pieces.

A mountainous wave tips the boat over and the sailors spill out.

1. Carib-Islands: the islands of the Caribbean Sea.
2. sandbar: a long, narrow sandbank.

Dragged under the waves, Robinson gasps for breath.

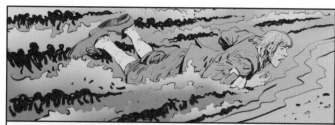

A wave carries him onto the sand…

…but before he can get away to safety, an even bigger wave pulls him back into the sea.

I can't believe it. My life is saved.

Robinson finally drags himself up the beach and out of danger.

Is there not one soul saved but myself?

There is no sign of the crew.

How is it possible that I could reach the shore alive?

Ah, sweet water!

He manages to find some fresh water to drink.

Fearing that he might be eaten by animals while he sleeps, he spends the night in a tree.

SCAVENGING SUPPLIES

By morning, the storm has calmed.

The ship is sitting upright on rocks near the shore.

Robinson swims out to see what he can salvage.[1]

He finds food in the ship's bread room.

I have need of a raft.

He builds a raft to carry supplies back from the ship.

This should keep me fed a while.

He finds three seamen's chests and fills them with food.

This fits me well.

He looks for clothes – the ones he left on the beach have been washed away.

Steady as she goes.

The rising tide and an onshore breeze help him back to the shore. The ship's dog swims ashore with him.

1. salvage: save from the wreckage.

The tide carries the raft up a creek.

Where to land?

Robinson finds a flat piece of ground to land the raft on.

He climbs a hill to get a better view of the land.

I am trapped on an island!

There seems to be food aplenty for the taking.

This will keep me safe tonight.

He piles up the chests to make a sort of hut.

There is time to make one more trip to the ship before nightfall.

He builds a second raft and loads it with more supplies.

Then he builds a shelter to cover anything that would be ruined by rain or sun.

What art thou good for?[1]

The supplies he finds on the ship include money – which is utterly useless to him now!

1. What art thou good for?: What use are you?

MOVING HOME

Robinson realises he will need a more secure home.

He finds the perfect place –

– a natural hollow at the foot of a rock.

He marks out the front wall of his new home.

He builds a strong wall by driving stakes into the ground.

He dismantles his old camp and moves the supplies to his new home.

To make his home secure, he enters and leaves by a ladder, not a door.

He pitches a tent on the plain and covers it with a tarpaulin.[1]

He hacks rock out of the hollow to make a small cave.

1. tarpaulin: a heavyweight waterproof cloth, made of tarred canvas in Robinson's time.

Fearing his gunpowder might be struck by lighting and explode, he divides it into small parcels and keeps them in different places. He uses his guns to hunt goats.

Oh, my powder!

I shall enjoy a dinner of the finest goat-meat!

He starts a calendar by cutting notches on a post.

In time, he builds a more permanent wooden roof for his home.

Although unskilled in carpentry, he makes a table and chair for himself.

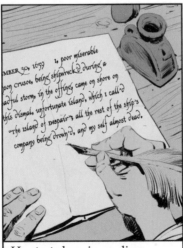

He starts keeping a diary.

He makes a lamp from a clay dish full of goat fat with some rope fibres as a wick.

EARTHQUAKE!

Robinson finds crops growing where he had emptied a bag of chicken feed.

Robinson finds crops growing where he had emptied a bag of chicken feed.

A violent earthquake strikes his island.

Rock falls from the roof of his cave and tumbles down the hill above it.

He finds a barrel of gunpowder washed up on the beach.

After a storm, pieces of the wreck of his ship are washed up further along the shore.

He spends more than a month cutting up the wreck and dragging the wood away.

He catches a turtle to eat.

It's a welcome change after eating only goat and birds.

Next day, he is seized by a fever. His body is racked by shivering, sweating and violent headaches.

The fever lasts ten days.

I shall ne'er[1] be short of fruit.

Recovered, he explores the island and discovers a fertile valley. Melons and grapevines grow in abundance.

He spends the night sleeping in a tree.

Such lush and verdant[2] growth!

The next day he discovers cocoa trees, then orange, lemon and lime trees.

A mightily wholesome[3] and refreshing drink.

He makes himself a fruit drink…

…and then returns with bags to collect more fruit.

These should furnish[4] my self for the wet season.

I shall dry these grapes to make raisins.

This will serve as my country house!

He builds himself a bower[5] in the valley.

Rain, rain and more rain.

Shall I ever leave this place?

He shelters in his cave during the rainy season. It rains nearly every day from August to October.

The notches on his calendar show he has been on the island exactly a year.

1. ne'er: never   2. verdant: green.   3, wholesome: healthy. An illness called scurvy was common among sailors at this time. It was later found to be due to a shortage of vitamin C, and was treated by adding citrus fruit (oranges, lemons, limes, etc.) to the diet.   4. furnish: supply.   5. bower: a woodland shelter made of branches.

FARMER CRUSOE

After the rains, Robinson sows barley and rice.

But his seeds fail to grow, because the soil has already dried out.

He sows more seeds in February, knowing that the rain will water them in March and April.

He tries his hand at making baskets.

Exploring more of his island, he sees land in the distance.

This side of the island is covered with grassland, woods and flowers.

He decides to keep a parrot as a pet.

On the seashore he finds turtles, animals running around, and birds in the trees.

After his exploration he returns home for a well-earned rest.

What with hunting and cooking, time passes quickly.

Robinson builds a fence to stop animals eating his crops.

He shoots several birds and hangs them over his land to scare the other birds away.

He makes a scythe[3] from a cutlass[4] to harvest his crops.

He sows all his seed on a new, bigger plot of land.

He teaches his parrot to say its name – the first word he has heard spoken in more than three years.

He digs clay to make pots…

…but the big ones crack as they dry out.

One piece of pottery falls into his cooking fire and is hardened by the heat.

Now he hardens and strengthens his clay pots by building a fire around them.

1. in solitary confinement: entirely alone (the phrase usually refers to imprisonment).   2. for a terror to the others: to frighten the other birds.   3. scythe: a hand tool with a curved blade to cut grass or grain crops.   4. cutlass: a short, broad slashing sword commonly used by sailors at this time.

A Near-Disaster

Robinson thinks about escaping from the island. He tries to turn the ship's boat the right way up, but it is too heavy to move.

He resolves to build a new boat by hollowing out a tree trunk.

It takes five months of hard work – and then he realises that he can't move it down to the water. It's too heavy!

The clothes he saved from the ship are worn out.

He makes a new suit of clothes from goat skins.

A goatskin umbrella keeps off the rain and the sun.

He builds a smaller, lighter boat and digs a channel to get it to the creek.

Success at last!

1. periagua (pe-ree-AG-wa): a dugout canoe.

He adds a mast, and a sail made from pieces of sail salvaged from the ship.

Now he sets out to sail around his island.

He plans to stay close to shore, because his new boat is too small to venture into the open sea.

But a strong current takes him out to sea!

Eventually the wind changes and delivers him, exhausted, back to the shore.

In the morning he continues round the coast, looking for a creek to let him sail inland.

He finds a convenient harbour for his boat and sets off on foot for home.

He rests at his bower in the fertile valley.

He wakes from a deep sleep to hear his name being called, as if in a dream – but it's only Poll, the parrot.

1. amply victualled: well supplied with food.
2. whither: where to?

A FOOTPRINT

With little powder left, Robinson's guns will soon be useless for hunting.

...but they easily bite through his snares.

Next, he digs deep pits to trap them.

He covers the pits with hurdles[1] and scatters food.

In the morning, he finds three kids – a male and two females – in one of his traps.

He has to drag them to their new home in the valley.

He tames the goats by feeding them from his hand.

He fences in part of the meadow to keep the goats in.

After two years he has a flock of 43 goats, which provide all the meat and milk he needs.

1. hurdles: panels made of thin, twiggy branches woven together.

What stares would I draw,[1] were I to travel through Yorkshire as I am?

He wonders what his fellow countrymen would make of him if they saw him dressed in his animal skins.

How can this be?

One morning he makes an astonishing discovery.

He dashes back to his cave, terrified that he might be attacked at any moment.

Such noises as I never heard before!

He lies awake all night. His imagination runs away with him. Ordinary noises fill him with dread.

He convinces himself that he must have made the footprint himself – but when he compares it to his foot, the footprint is much bigger.

The footprint is not mine!

I must erase all signs of my presence from the land.

He decides to destroy his crops, animal pens and fences to hide his existence.

No, I will hide myself from the eyes of visitors.

In the morning he changes his mind: he will just take care not to be seen by anyone.

I will be safe as if in a fortress.

He fortifies his home by building a strong outer wall and setting up his muskets[2] ready to be fired through it at any attackers.

1. What stares would I draw?: What strange looks would people give me?
2. muskets: guns with a long barrel, fired from the shoulder.

CANNIBALS!

Horror!

One day, Robinson makes a grisly discovery on the beach. His island has been visited by cannibals![1]

I must show a fierce bearing[2] to my enemies.

He tries to look as tough, fearsome and well-armed as possible, to scare off anyone thinking of attacking him.

The smoke from my fire could give me away.

This will fit my purpose.

He finds a big cave where he can light a fire safely…

…but he is not alone!

Be this a devil or a man?

Returning with a torch, he finds that the eyes belong to a goat too ill even to stand up.

Frighted by a sick he-goat!

Next day, he moves supplies into his new cave.

My visitors are returned.

Early one morning, he spots the light of a fire on the shore. The natives are making regular visits to the island.

1. cannibals: people who eat human flesh.
2. a fierce bearing: a frightening appearance.

Is that a cannon I hear fired at sea?

BOOM!

During a fierce storm one night, Robinson hears a noise that is not thunder.

Is there a ship in the night?

He hopes the passing ship will see his fire.

I am to be rescued!

BOOM!

BOOM!

But in the morning he finds the ship stuck fast on the rocks.

O that there had been but one soul saved!

The cannon was a distress signal!

He sails out to the ship, a Spanish vessel.

A new companion!

A dog eagerly jumps down from the deck.

I would give it all for a pair of English shoes and stockings.

There are no other survivors. He quickly collects anything useful.

He finds a fortune in gold, but it is as worthless to him as the dirt on the ground.

Perhaps it is time to show some courage and sail away.

Rather than fall into the hands of cannibals, he thinks it may be time to try to escape from the island.

FRIDAY

One morning, Robinson discovers 30 natives on the beach – far too many for him to fight off if they see him.

They have two prisoners. One breaks free.

The prisoner swims across a creek, followed by two of his captors.

As the prisoner runs past, Robinson steps out and knocks the first native to the ground with the stock of his gun.

The second native aims an arrow at Robinson, who shoots him dead.

The prisoner shows his gratitude to Robinson for saving his life.

As the first native comes to, the prisoner kills him with Robinson's sword.

The prisoner quickly buries the bodies so they will not be found.

Robinson gives the prisoner food and water in his cooking cave.

He names the prisoner after the day when he saved him.

You Friday. Me Master.[1]

You are almost as well clothed as your Master.

Friday, this is where you will sleep.

Robinson gives Friday new clothes and makes a place for him to sleep.

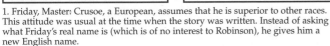

BANG!

Friday is terrified by the noise of Robinson's gun.

Robinson later sees Friday talking to the gun.

I believe he would worship it!

He is begging it not to kill him.

Robinson teaches Friday to speak English.

He shows him how to farm the land and look after the animals.

1. Friday, Master: Crusoe, a European, assumes that he is superior to other races. This attitude was usual at the time when the story was written. Instead of asking what Friday's real name is (which is of no interest to Robinson), he gives him a new English name.

A NEW BOAT

Friday, are your people's canoes often lost at sea?

No, canoes go with current in the morning and come home with current in afternoon.

Robinson quizzes Friday about his people's travels on the ocean.

I know where we are!

Robinson realises that Friday is talking about tides washing in and out of the great Orinoco river.[1]

There, beyond the moon,[2] white-beard mans like you.

Can we go to these men?

Yes, yes, in two canoe.[3]

This is the boat that brought me here.

Me see such boat at my nation.

We save the white mans from drown in boat like this.

They must be from the ship cast away[4] in sight of my island.

Friday thinks they can reach the place where the white-bearded men live.

Robinson shows Friday the remains of the ship's boat.

Friday, do you wish yourself in your own nation?

I be much glad to be at my own nation.

Such a boat carry much vittle.[5]

But the wood is split and rotten.

But your boat too small.

Friday, I have a bigger boat.

Robinson remembers the bigger boat he built years earlier – but it is in a poor state now.

1. Orinoco river: one of the longest rivers in South America, in present-day Venezuela and Colombia.
2. beyond the moon: in the west, where the moon sets.   3. two canoe: a large boat the size of two canoes.
4. cast away: wrecked.   5. vittel: victuals (food and other provisions).

Friday thinks he has done something wrong and is being sent away.

Why you angry mad with Friday? Why send Friday home?

No, no, Friday, I go too.

They start building a new boat.

This tree make good periagua.

It takes them a month to finish their new boat, and two weeks to push and drag it to the water.

She floats!

Robinson teaches Friday how to sail the boat.

This stout roof will keep the rain off our boat.

They build a small dock to store the boat in until the weather is fair to leave.

AN ENGLISH SHIP

Friday, see if you can find us a turtle on the seashore.

At the end of the rainy season, Robinson and Friday lay in supplies for their voyage.

Friday spots a ship anchored near the island.

Master, they are come!

An English ship!

Eight sailors bring three prisoners ashore in a longboat.[1]

While the guards sleep, the prisoners are shocked to see a wild, fur-clad man creeping up to them.

Gentlemen, do not be surprised at me.

I am the ship's commander. My crew has mutinied.[2]

Let us retreat out of their hearing, lest they awake.

If I venture upon your deliverance,[3] will you carry me and my man[4] to England?

Robinson offers to help the captain if he will take him and Friday to England. The captain agrees.

Here are three muskets for you, with powder and ball.[5]

Robinson arms the prisoners with guns from his store.

1. longboat: an open boat with oars and a sail, carried on board a ship.   2. mutinied: taken control of the ship and made the captain their prisoner.   3. If I venture upon your deliverance: If I take the risk of rescuing you. 4. my man: my servant.   5. powder and ball: gunpowder and lead bullets.

The leaders of the mutiny must not be allowed to escape.

The mutineers wake to find the captain almost upon them.

Rouse yourselves!

Swear your allegiance to me[1] and I will spare your miserable lives.

Another longboat is sent ashore to see what has happened.

They have firearms with them.

When the new arrivals call out to their companions, Friday answers them.

Hollow![2]

Hollow!

He leads the mutineers all over the island following the sound of his voice.

Hollow! Hollow!

This is truly a land of demons and spirits.

The exhausted men surrender, believing that the island is haunted.

The captain and some of his crew row out to the ship and board it.

BLAM!

When the leading mutineer is shot dead, the captain is once again in command of his ship.

---

1. Swear your allegiance to me: Promise to follow my orders.   2. Hollow: Hello there.

Coming Home

The captain gives Robinson a suit of English clothes. They feel very strange!

Two of the ringleaders decide to stay on the island rather than face execution.

Stay here and keep your lives, or leave with us in irons and go to the gallows.[1]

Robinson keeps his goatskin cap, his umbrella and one of his parrots.

19 December 1686

Finally, I am bound for England!

Robinson leaves the island behind after 28 years, 2 months and 19 days.[2]

I am as perfect a stranger to all the world as if I had never been known here.

Back in England, everything has changed. His friends have all gone.

You owe me nothing.[3]

The captain's widow has fallen on hard times. He helps her all he can.

In York, he learns that his parents are dead, but finds two sisters and two nephews.

He travels to Lisbon in Portugal, for news of his plantation in Brazil.[4]

Your plantation has prospered.

Can this really all be mine?

Robinson's partner in Brazil sends him the profit from his plantation.

---

116   1. go to the gallows: be hanged for mutiny.   2. 28 years, 2 months and 19 days: Robinson's arithmetic is wrong! He was shipwrecked on 30 September 1659 (see his calendar sign on page 99), so he has been there 27 years, 2 months and 19 days. 3. You owe me nothing: You need not return the money you were keeping for me.   4. Portugal, Brazil: Brazil was a Portuguese colony at this time; it became independent in 1822.

Robinson is so dazed by the news of his new wealth that a doctor has to be called.

He has a fortune of more than £5,000 in coin and a large estate in Brazil.

Robinson sets off for England on horseback with Friday and a group of other travellers.

It seems I am a rich man.

The patient will recover with a little bloodletting.[1]

In the Pyrenees,[2] Friday sees snow for the first time and is afraid of it.

What is this that makes my skin hurt?

It's called snow.

Their guide is attacked by wolves. Friday shoots one of the wolves, which scares the others away.

O Master! O Master!

A bear walks out of the wood onto the path. Friday taunts it fearlessly before killing it.

You fool, he will eat you up!

Me shakee te hand with him! Me make you good laugh.

On English soil again, Robinson sells his Brazilian estate for a princely sum.

What an uncommon adventure I have had!

1. bloodletting: slitting open a vein to let blood trickle out. In earlier centuries this was believed to be a cure for many different illnesses.   2. Pyrenees: a range of mountains on the border between Spain and France.

The end

ROBERT LOUIS STEVENSON (1850–1894)

Robert Louis Stevenson was born in Edinburgh, Scotland, on 13 November 1850. He was the only son of Thomas Stevenson and his wife Margaret Isabella Balfour. Both families were wealthy, well educated and deeply respectable. Robert's mother suffered from tuberculosis, and it is unclear whether she passed the disease on to him, or whether he suffered from another lung disorder. Either way, he was often too ill to attend school, and so lay in bed, reading or composing poems and stories of his own.

UNIVERSITY

Aged 17, he enrolled at Edinburgh University. His father wanted him to study engineering, but Robert wasn't keen; he wanted to be a writer. As a compromise he studied law, but spent all his spare time writing. During holidays he travelled to France to meet other young artists and writers. He was often ill, but always lively-minded, unconventional and determined.

MARRIAGE

Robert qualified as a lawyer in 1875, but never worked in the profession. His first book, about a canoeing expedition in France, was published in 1878, and he spent the rest of his life as a writer. In France, Robert also met the woman who would later become his wife: Fanny Van de Grift Osbourne, an American. They were a strange couple, but passionately in love. She was everything he was not: loud, healthy and vibrant. Robert's family were not happy, because Fanny was 11 years older than Robert, and was already married. In 1880, after Fanny's divorce, Robert travelled to America to marry her. Robert's family were appalled, but the couple were happy together.

FIRST NOVEL

In 1881 Robert and Fanny travelled to Scotland with Fanny's son, Lloyd Osbourne. They made peace with Robert's family, and visited the Highlands with them. But the cold and rain worsened Robert's health. Then, in 1883, he published his first long novel. Its title was *Treasure Island*. During the next six years Robert wrote four more novels. These included his most famous work, *The Strange Case of Dr Jekyll and Mr Hyde*. This brilliant fantasy thriller was an instant bestseller and made him famous throughout Britain and America.

DETERIORATING HEALTH

By 1887 Robert's health was getting worse, so he and Fanny returned to America with his mother (his father had died). Then with Fanny's children they set sail across the Pacific Ocean.

SAMOA

After a long voyage they settled on the island of Samoa. They built a house and made friends with the islanders, who called Robert 'Tusitala' ('Teller of Tales'). Robert was fascinated by the islands and their rich heritage of songs and stories. He collected information for a huge history of the Pacific, campaigned to stop Europeans ill-treating local people, and wrote poems and stories about the island. Robert also wrote novels set in faraway Scotland. The last of these, *Weir of Hermiston*, which he never finished, was probably his best piece of writing.

Sadly, even the warm Pacific climate could not cure Robert's illness, and he died suddenly on 3 December 1894; he was just 44 years old. He was buried on the top of Mount Vaea, above his home in Samoa, and lines from his own poem 'Requiem' were carved on his tomb:

Under the wide and starry sky,
Dig the grave and let me lie.
Glad did I live and gladly die,
And I laid me down with a will.

HERMAN MELVILLE (1819–1891)

Herman Melville was born on 1st August, 1819, in New York. His father, Allan Melville, was an import merchant trading in such items as handkerchiefs, scarves and ribbons. His business was not thriving, but Allan was a dreamer who continually believed success was just around the corner and frequently moved his family into larger and larger houses to make it appear that business was booming. Finally, in October 1830, with his business in ruins, the Melville family (with eight children) travelled to Albany, New York state, where Allan was forced to beg his brother-in-law for financial help.

EDUCATION
In 1832, Allan caught pneumonia. His delirium in the final days before his death is thought to have inspired the image of Captain Ahab raving in his hammock. After this, Herman and his elder brother, Gansevoort, stopped attending school and were sent out to work to support their family. It wasn't thought a terrible loss for Herman's schooling to end – he was a terrible speller and was not considered an outstanding student. From this point on, he was self-educated. After a failed attempt to become a surveyor and a brief spell as a teacher, Melville returned to New York feeling restless and in search of adventure.

SEA TRAVELS
On 5th June, 1839, Melville set sail for Liverpool, England on the *St Lawrence*. The crew list contains an entry for a 'Norman Melville' – possibly a result of his poor handwriting. It was then that he decided to join the crew of a whaling ship. He set out for New Bedford and on 3rd January 1841, set sail on the *Acushnet*, a whaler bound for the Pacific Ocean. In July 1841 the *Acushnet* arrived at Nukuheva in the South Pacific. Melville promptly deserted and spent a month there in the Typee Valley. Typee warriors were ferocious and there were rumours of cannibalism. Their bodies were covered with tattoos marking battle victories, and it is possible this experience inspired the character of tattooed harpooner, Queequeg.
Melville then joined the crew of an Australian whaler, arrived in Tahiti in September 1842, and was promptly imprisoned as a mutineer.

Released after a few weeks, Melville continued his travels before finally returning to America in 1844.

MELVILLE, THE WRITER
Upon his return home, Melville delighted his friends and family with tales of his adventures and set about writing them down for a wider audience. His first novel, *Typee*, was rejected by American publishers because it was thought too fantastic to be true, so Gansevoort took it to London in search of a publisher. He succeeded, and *Typee* was published in England in March 1846 and America in August of the same year.

MOBY-DICK
Melville had first heard an account of a real whaling ship tragedy while aboard the *Acushnet*. The *Essex* had been rammed and sunk by a large sperm whale in 1820 and Melville drew upon Owen Chase's account of his survival while writing *Moby-Dick*. He had also heard reports of an old albino whale named Mocha Dick (named after the island of Mocha near Chile). This white whale was said to repeatedly turn and attack its hunters. *Moby-Dick* was published in 1851. In Britain it was split into three volumes entitled *The Whale*, in America it was published as a single novel called *Moby-Dick* or *The Whale*.[1]

AFTER *MOBY-DICK*
In spite of his reputation today as one of America's finest writers, Herman Melville only wrote in the years from 1845 to 1857. Sadly he never achieved the critical or financial success as a writer he hoped for, and in later life turned to writing poems, many of which were unpublished during his lifetime. From 1857, money problems caused Melville to seek a living on the lecture circuit. However, he had a very quiet speaking voice, and after three years he gave it up. Melville's later years were marked by great personal tragedy. Both his sons died before him: Malcolm shot himself in 1867 and Stanwix died in 1886. His final novel, *Billy Budd*, was unfinished when he died in 1891 and remained unpublished until 1924.

1. The original title of the novel is hyphenated, although the whale's name throughout is not.

Daniel Defoe (c.1660–1731)

D aniel Defoe was born in London in about the year 1660. His name at birth was Daniel Foe, and his parents were Alice and James Foe. His parents were dissenters (Christians who had broken away from the Church of England), and young Daniel was brought up as a dissenter. By 1683 he had become a general merchant, selling hosiery, woollen goods, tobacco and wine. He travelled extensively throughout England and Europe in the course of his business.

In 1684 Foe married Mary Tuffley. Daniel and Mary had eight children, six of whom survived.

The year after they were married, Foe joined the Monmouth Rebellion, an attempt to overthrow the newly crowned King James II. The rebellion failed and most of its participants were executed or transported to the Americas; Foe was lucky to escape punishment.

Money worries

In 1692 Foe was arrested because of unpaid debts, which may have been as high as £17,000 (worth more than half a million pounds today), and declared bankrupt. After a series of different jobs, he set up a brick and tile factory in Tilbury, Essex. Around 1695 he started calling himself De Foe, which later became Defoe. Two years later, he wrote *An Essay on Projects*, which proposed a variety of social and economic reforms for banks, insurance societies, asylums, roads and schools.

In the early 1700s he turned his attention to politics and religion. It wasn't long before his views landed him in trouble. In 1703 he was arrested for writing an inflammatory pamphlet called *The Shortest Way with the Dissenters*. After three days in the pillory he was sent to London's Newgate Prison. While he was in prison, his factory went out of business and he was bankrupt again. After six months, he received a pardon thanks to Robert Harley, the Speaker of the House of Commons. In return for his release, Defoe agreed to work as a spy for Harley. At the same time, he was also writing political news sheets and pamphlets.

The great storm

In 1704 Defoe wrote his first book, *The Storm*. It was a collection of first-hand accounts of the Great Storm of 1703. This is reputed to have been the worst storm ever to hit the British Isles. About 8,000 sailors died as their ships were wrecked and sunk in the North Sea. On land, whole rows of houses were levelled, 400 windmills were destroyed, a million trees were blown over and many churches lost their spires and towers.

In the same year, Defoe started writing *The Review*, a paper that was published three times a week. Its contents included news and essays on government policy and trade, and articles on manners and morals. Defoe wrote all of it himself.

Fame

In 1713 and 1714 Defoe was arrested on several occasions because of his political writings and further unpaid debts. In 1719 his most famous book was published. Now known simply as *Robinson Crusoe*, its full title was: *The Life and Strange Surprizing Adventures of Robinson Crusoe, of York, Mariner: Who lived Eight and Twenty Years, all alone in an un-inhabited Island on the coast of America, near the Mouth of the Great River of Oroonoque; Having been cast on Shore by Shipwreck, where-in all the Men perished but himself. With An Account how he was at last as strangely deliver'd by Pyrates. Written by Himself.*

Defoe continued to publish successful novels, including *Memoirs of a Cavalier*, *Colonel Jack*, *Moll Flanders* and *The Life, Adventures and Piracies of the Famous Captain Singleton*. He also wrote travel books, including *A Voyage Round the World* and *A Tour Thro' the Whole Island of Great Britain*. And he wrote books on personal conduct and behaviour, including *The Family Instructor* and *The Compleat English Gentleman*. He even wrote about ghosts, including *An Essay on the History and Reality of Apparitions*. *A Journal of the Plague Year* is a history of the Great Plague of 1665, written as though it were an eyewitness account.

By 1724 Defoe was quite wealthy again. He had a large house with stables and grounds built for himself at Stoke Newington, London. He appears to have had property elsewhere too. But by the time of his death, on 24 April 1731, he was once again suffering from money trouble. He died at lodgings in Ropemaker's Alley in Moorfields, London, and was buried at Bunhill Fields. No-one knows how he lost his wealth, or why he did not die at home.